"If I had read this when I was eighteen, it would have saved me a lot of heartache. This is a great guide, handbook, blueprint, road map, compass, trail, and foundation for life. Read it for yourself, and give it to your children."

—Stephen Arterburn, cofounder,
Minirth-Meier New Life Clinics

"The wisdom of the Bible is designed to reveal the underlying moral and spiritual realities God has built into His creation. Max Anders has tapped into that wisdom to spell out for us some of the ways things work in God's world. Always readable and well-illustrated, 21 Unbreakable Laws of Life *will help more than a few readers avoid some divinely placed brick walls and find the way God wills them to take."*

—Duane Litfin, president,
Wheaton College

"If you want to be a healthy, balanced Christian—this book holds the keys."

—Rick Warren, pastor,
Saddleback Valley Community Church

"Max Anders gives you a working knowledge of life's non-negotiables and a proven plan to turn them into 'second nature' traits in your heart."

—Tim Kimmel, author,
Little House on the Freeway

"Max has done it again! 21 Unbreakable Laws of Life *is must reading. Simple, clear, biblical, entertaining, convicting, and life-changing. I teach a class on the spiritual life. I've just discovered an excellent text for the course. Max's insights, authenticity, and practicality make the book a ten-plus. I thoroughly and completely endorse it."*

Joe C. Aldrich, president,
Multnomah Bible College and Seminary

Other books by Max Anders:

The Holy Spirit: Knowing Our Comforter
The Bible: Embracing God's Truth
Jesus: Knowing Our Savior
God: Knowing Our Creator
Spiritual Warfare: Winning the Invisible War
The Church: Finding Your Place in the Body of Christ
30 Days to Understanding the Bible
30 Days to Understanding How to Live as a Christian
30 Days to Understanding What Christians Believe

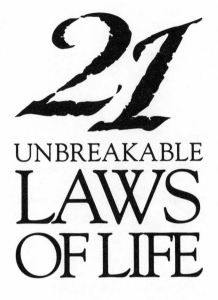

21
UNBREAKABLE
LAWS
OF LIFE

MAX ANDERS

THOMAS NELSON PUBLISHERS
Nashville • Atlanta • London • Vancouver

Published in Nashville, Tennessee, by Thomas Nelson, Inc., and distributed in Canada by Word Communications, Ltd., Richmond, British Columbia, and in the United Kingdom by Word (UK), Ltd., Milton Keynes, England.

Excerpt from "The Last Great Race" in *Winterdance: The Fine Madness of Running the Iditarod*, copyright © 1994 by Gary Paulsen, reprinted by permission of Harcourt Brace & Company.

Unless otherwise noted, Scripture quotations are from the NEW KING JAMES VERSION of the Bible. Copyright © 1979, 1980, 1982, 1990, 1994, Thomas Nelson, Inc., Publishers.

Scripture quotations noted TEV are from the *Good News Bible*, Old Testament © 1976 by the American Bible Society; New Testament © 1966, 1971, 1976 American Bible Society. Used by permission.

Library of Congress Cataloging-in-Publication Data

Anders, Max E., 1947–
    21 unbreakable laws of life / Max Anders.
        p. cm.
    Includes bibliographical references.
    ISBN 0-7852-7611-4
    1. Christian life—Study and teaching. I. Title.
BV4511.A73 1996
248.4—dc20
                                                                    96-10659
                                                                    CIP

Printed in the United States of America
1 2 3 4 5 6 7 - 02 01 00 99 98 97 96

This book is dedicated to the memory of my sister, Marcia, whom we all loved and miss, but who is now in better hands.

Contents

Acknowledgments

I would like to acknowledge the people who helped make this book possible.

I am grateful to my wife, Margie, who is my most loyal supporter and gifted evaluator. I am grateful to my family and friends who encouraged me to pursue the idea of the book.

Mike Hyatt and Robert Wolgemuth helped sharpen the concept and guide the project.

At Thomas Nelson, Bruce Nygren saw possibilities in the book and gave it his gifted editorial attention. Leslie Peterson improved the manuscript with her skilled copyediting and her faithful and gracious attention to detail.

I am grateful to you all.

Introduction

Life can be a jungle. Its overgrown paths are often uncharted, dangers lurk around every bend, and it always rains when you don't want it to. But if you know the rules, things will always go better.

If life actually *were* a jungle, here are some laws that might be helpful:

1. Never turn your back on a skinny lion.

2. Don't try to reason with a cobra.

3. Always run perpendicular to stampeding elephants.

4. Never take a nap on an anthill.

5. If vultures are circling above you, see a doctor soon.

6. Don't get uppity with a rhinoceros.

7. If you can smell a snake, it's too late.

8. Covering your head in bed at night doesn't really help, but it will make you feel better.

9. Don't try to perspire. Just let go and sweat.

10. L.L. Bean can keep you warm in the Arctic but not cool in the jungle.

11. If you're in a group that meets a lion, you don't have to outrun the lion, just the slowest member of your group.

12. Don't be fooled by the sound of helicopters. It's really mosquitoes.

13. Hyenas can be dangerous. If you come upon a pack, quickly tell a good joke. It will immobilize them for several minutes while you get away.

14. When building a tree house, don't use any "limbs" that move.

15. Don't eat bananas every day. Even if you like them, you'll soon get sick of them.

16. Don't mess with warthogs. They're tougher than they look.

17. There's safety in numbers. When lions are on the prowl, get in a herd of wildebeest and put a stupid expression on your face.

18. Don't try to help a giraffe with a sore throat. The condition is beyond your ability to remedy.

19. The same is true of an elephant with a head cold.

20. The same is true of a boa constrictor with a slipped disk.

21. To stop a charging elephant, cut up its credit cards.

These laws might make you smile, but just as there are real laws of the jungle you will pay a terrible price for violating, so there are laws of life, and you will pay a terrible price for violating them. Someone has said that you cannot break the laws of God. . . . You can only break yourself against them when you violate them. I think that's true.

When planning a trip through the jungle, it is helpful to have a handbook, a pocket guide that gives a brief synopsis of key information you might already know but need to be sure not to forget. That's the purpose of this book—to remind you of things you might already know but might lose sight of as you thrash your way through the jungle of life. Each of these laws will save you pain, keep you on course, and lighten your load. Keep them and thrive. Violate them and suffer. Life goes better when you follow the rules.

1

The Law of Happiness:
An Unexpected Gift

Happiness isn't found by pursuing it;
it is a by-product of pursuing God.

In Your presence is fullness of joy;
At Your right hand are pleasures forevermore.
Psalm 16:11

I once heard of a man who was unhappy in his work, unhappy with his family, and unhappy with life in general, so he decided to escape to get away from it all. He joined a mute monastery, where he took a vow of silence. He could say only two words every five years.

This is perfect, he thought. *No stress, no one to bug me, nothing but silence.*

So he stayed there five years without uttering a syllable. At the end of that time, his superior called the man into his office and said, "You have two words you can speak. Would you like to say anything?"

The guy nodded his head and said, "Bad food!"

He went for another five years without uttering a syllable, and again his superior called him into his office and asked if he would like to say anything.

He nodded his head and said, "Hard bed!"

Another five years passed, and his superior called him in and asked him if he would like to say anything, and the guy said, "I quit!"

His superior responded, "Well, I'm not surprised. You've done nothing but complain since you got here!"

What do most people want out of life?
Most people say they want to be happy.

When you ask most people what they want out of life they say they want to be happy. They have different ideas as to what it would take to make them happy, but everyone pursues happiness. Some pursue it in wealth. Others pursue it in poverty. But all pursue happiness. Blaise Pascal, a seventeenth century philosopher, once wrote:

All men seek happiness. This is without exception. Whatever different means they employ, they all tend to this end. The cause of some going to war and of others avoiding it, is the same desire in both, attending with different views. The will never takes the least step but to this objective. This is the motive of every man, even of those who hang themselves.[1]

As Christians, we may be vaguely uncomfortable admitting happiness is a priority for us. It doesn't sound spiritual. Yet the Bible doesn't seem to shy away from presenting happiness as a valid longing:

> As the deer pants for the water brooks,
> So pants my soul for You, O God.
> My soul thirsts for God, for the living God. (Ps. 42:1-2)

> O God, You are my God;
> Early will I seek You;
> My soul thirsts for You;
> My flesh longs for You
> In a dry and thirsty land
> Where there is no water. (Ps. 63:1)

> You will show me the path of life;
> In Your presence is fullness of joy;
> At Your right hand are pleasures forevermore. (Ps. 16:11)

In these verses the Bible speaks of deep longings we have and implies that the fulfillment of these longings, as well as joy and pleasure, are things God does not find objectionable in humanity. Rather, He seems to encourage it, as long as our pursuit of happiness is centered in Him.

There is an old and highly regarded church document, the Westminster Confession, which states that the chief end of man is to glorify God and enjoy Him forever. *Is that true?* we ask ourselves. *Can we enjoy God? Will we be able to enjoy Him forever?* Well, if the Bible is true, the answer is yes!

How can we be happy?
By pursuing God, and trusting Him for happiness.

If happiness for us comes only through maintaining a sufficient flow of favorable circumstances, life will be pretty hard on most of us. First, we cannot be happy merely with pleasurable circumstances. Pleasurable circumstances make good frosting but not a good cake. Second, even if circumstances *could* make us happy, we cannot control them adequately enough to bring us consistent happiness.

If happiness for us comes only through maintaining a sufficient flow of favorable circumstances, life will be pretty hard on most of us.

A prime example of this is found in Charles Kuralt's book, *A Life on the Road.* Kuralt for many years was host of *Sunday Morning,* a weekly television program, and host of *On the Road* specials on CBS in which he traveled around the United States in a motor home and filmed interesting stories about unusual people or happenings. Portions of his work often aired on *The CBS Evening News with Walter Cronkite.* Every evening when Cronkite, one of the most respected men in America, completed his newscast he signed off in his distinctive voice and style, "And that's the way it is." It was one of the most famous phrases in America for decades. Kuralt wrote:

> A woman wrote me a letter from Ohio. She said her parakeet could say "And that's the way it is" like Walter Cronkite. We went there right away, of course. As soon as she opened the door, the parakeet said, "And that's the way it is." While we set up the lights and camera there in the living room, the parakeet watched us from the inside of his cage and said, "And that's the way it is!" We pointed the lens at the cage and started rolling. The parakeet looked at the camera and said:
>
> "Aaaawk!"
>
> The parakeet's owner said, "And that's the way it is!" to give him a cue.

The parakeet said, "Aaaaawk!"

"And that's the way it is!" she said patiently.

He said, "Aaaaaaawk!"

We turned off the lights to let the parakeet calm down. We went into the kitchen and had a cup of coffee and talked about the weather and other things. Then we sauntered back into the living room, and pretended to pay no attention to the parakeet in his cage. The bird's owner thought this might work. We said nothing. The parakeet said nothing. We turned on the camera again.

The parakeet said, "Aaaaawk!"

After an hour or two of this, we packed up, promising to return some other time. We said good-bye to the disappointed woman who wanted to see her parakeet on Walter Cronkite's news program. We closed the front door and started down the walk to the driveway, carrying our camera and lights. Behind us in the living room, we heard the parakeet say:

"And that's the way it is!"[2]

And that *is* the way it is. You try to control circumstances, and you can't.

Solomon told us this 2,000 years ago, but we don't quite believe him. Solomon, the son of David, was probably handsome enough to be a male model. He was wealthier than perhaps any man alive today. He was commander in chief of a powerful army and king of a great nation. He was brilliant.

With all this going for him, Solomon admitted that he did not withhold anything from himself. If he wanted it, he got it. He lived a rich, full life in the terms of this world. But as an old man, he said that all the things this world had to offer were unsatisfying. In the end, he wrote, "Let us hear the conclusion of the whole matter: / Fear God and keep His commandments, / For this is man's all" (Ecc. 12:13).

Our problem is that we don't quite believe Solomon. We think that for some unknown reason, he just didn't get it right. Yes, he had brains, money, looks, fame, and power and wasn't happy, but if *we* had brains, money, looks, fame, and power, *we* would be happy. We would be able to pull it off.

In *Life, Liberty and the Pursuit of Happiness,* Peggy Noonan, former speech writer for Presidents Reagan and Bush, wrote:

> It is a terrible thing when people lose God. Life is difficult and people are afraid, and to be without God is to lose man's great source of consolation and coherence.
>
> I think we have lost the old knowledge that happiness is over-rated—that, in a way, life is overrated. We have lost somehow a sense of mystery—about us, our purpose, our meaning, our role. Our ancestors believed in two worlds, and understood this to be the solitary, poor, nasty, brutish and short one. We are the first generations of man that actually expected to find happiness here on earth, and our search for it has caused such unhappiness. The reason: if you do not believe in another, higher world, if you believe only in the flat material world around you, if you believe that this is your only chance at happiness—if that is what you believe, then you are more than disappointed when the world does not give you a good measure of its riches, you are in despair.[3]

Our ability to be happy in this life is greatly increased by the knowledge that complete happiness can be found only in the next life.

So true! If we pursue happiness in what this temporal world alone has to offer us, then life can be a profound disappointment. Pursue God and the fullness of the life He offers, and happiness dawns like the sun after a dark night. Our ability to be happy in this life is greatly increased by the knowledge that complete happiness can be found only in the next life.

How can we cultivate greater capacity for happiness?
By being grateful for the things God has given us, rather than ungrateful for what He has not given us.

Once we have laid a foundation for happiness by putting God at the center of our lives, we gain daily happiness largely by taking pleasure out of the little things in life rather than demanding a succession of big things. If only big things make us happy, we won't have a very happy life. When I think back over my life to remember the big things that made me happy, there are not many that still impress me today. I remember when I found a publisher for my first book. I whooped and danced and skipped around like a child. The happiness lasted for a couple of days. Then I was faced with the daunting task of finishing the book. Happiness from things like that lasts a few hours, a few days, or a few weeks. Then often it's gone.

If you added up all the time you were happy from the big things, you would be lucky to be happy for a year out of your whole life. But if you allow yourself to be happy over little things, happiness becomes a much more frequent visitor. Let me mention a few of the things that make me happy:

- my wife's smile
- the cardinal at my bird feeder
- the delicate lemon-yellow daylilies that bloom in July
- the stuff I got to clean the white sidewalls on my tires that actually worked
- a blue sky on a clear day
- the different colors of green in the new growth of spring
- two babies looking at each other in amazement at the grocery store checkout line
- the smell of dinner cooking
- the sound of a child's laughter
- a photograph of good friends
- a recording of music I like
- returning the wave of someone I see while I'm driving
- the taste of fresh fruit in season
- an unexpected phone call from a friend
- the chiming of a windup clock that I like
- watching friends and family meeting at the airport
- the stained-glass windows in the fancy church on Main Street

- a golden retriever puppy
- a postcard from a friend on vacation
- moonlight shimmering on the lake
- my wife and I getting our baked-potato soup recipe just right
- the sight of a horse grazing in a field
- the architecture of the courthouse in my hometown
- a nearby field of wildflowers
- grilling hamburgers with friends and helping their boys fish off the end of the pier

Sometime back I began to develop the habit of imagining what life would be like without the various things I enjoy. Imagine what life would be like without food, clothing, and shelter. Imagine if you had to fear someone kicking the door in and finding you worshipping. Imagine if you did not have anyone to love you or anyone to love. Imagine if you lost the freedoms guaranteed in the Constitution. Imagine what life would be like if you didn't have little things to brighten your life.

This practice helped me in three ways:

1. It made me more *aware* of the things I liked.

2. It made me more *appreciative* of them.

3. It increased my capacity for happiness.

I am so deeply grateful that I can see, hear, smell, touch, and taste. I am so grateful I can read. I am so grateful for my wife, my family, and my friends. I am so grateful I live in a country where the Bible is readily available, where I can worship as I please. I am so grateful I don't have to worry about where my next meal is coming from. I am so grateful for electricity so I can read at night, listen to classical music, and toast a bagel before I go to bed. I am so grateful when I get up in the morning and I am not in pain. I am so grateful I love people, and there are people who love me.

Joy in life depends on accepting the will of God in our lives and focusing on God's love, what He has done for us, is doing for us, and will do for us. Joy depends on enjoying the salvation brought to us in Jesus and knowing all our ultimate needs in life have already been met, and God will see us through the hard times. Joy depends on serving Jesus, telling others about Him, knowing God has chosen to use our feeble efforts to advance His kingdom.

If you allow yourself to be happy
over little things, happiness becomes
a much more frequent visitor.

But *happiness* in life, I believe, depends on cultivating the ability to notice and appreciate the ordinary things in life, and realizing that if you didn't have them, they wouldn't seem so ordinary. When we're in a crisis, it's hard to glean happiness from the ordinary things. Our world shrinks until it is just us and the crisis. But when the crisis passes, happiness in life depends on appreciating the little things. The big things don't come along often enough to keep us happy. But there is no end to the little things.

Happiness is a gift to those who follow God's truth.

I don't think it's accurate to say that only Christians can know happiness. That is clearly not the case. Some non-Christians are happier than some Christians. In addition, there are those who by natural temperament seem happy whether or not they are Christians. However, it is equally true there is much unhappiness in this world, and those who violate God's laws of life to the greatest measure experience the brunt of it. Regardless of whether someone believes in the Bible, its principles work. Faith, hope, love, honesty, industry, chastity, and all the other virtues in the Bible yield a richness, a satisfaction, a happiness that cannot be found in a life devoid of them.

The *surest* road to happiness is living for God, placing our ultimate hope in the next world, and learning to be grateful for the small things that come our way in this world.

Life-Check

1. What do you think of the statement, "The chief end of mankind is to glorify God by enjoying Him forever"? Does it ring true to you?

2. How would you evaluate Peggy Noonan's statement that happiness is overrated and we need to refocus on the "higher world" as the ultimate source of happiness?

3. What are the little, ordinary things in life that give you happiness? How do you think you could expand your list?

For Further Reflection

Scripture (Some Bibles use "blessed" instead of "happy.")
John 13:17
Psalm 42:2
Psalm 63:1-2
Psalm 16:11
Proverbs 16:20
Proverbs 17:1
Galatians 5:22-23

Book
Joy That Lasts, Gary Smally

2

The Law of Holiness:

The Right Way to Live Is to Live Right

The key to living a holy life is
"ready repentance" of sin.

As He who called you is holy,
you also be holy in all your conduct,
because it is written, "Be holy, for I am holy."
1 Peter 1:15-16

*I*was in big trouble. It was Friday afternoon, and I desperately needed a haircut. I didn't have enough time to go to my regular barber, so I called a large establishment near my home, the one where the sign said they cut both men and women's hair. They said they could get me in right away.

I jumped in the car and took off. As I was driving, a sense of foreboding came rolling over me like fog off a swamp. The memory of bad haircuts at the hands of new barbers flashed back vividly.

I parked the car and walked toward the front door. I don't remember the name of the place but, for reasons that will become clear, I refer to it now as *Delilah's Den*.

As soon as I walked in, I knew that my darkest fears would be realized. The air was thick with perfume. Heavy, sensual music throbbed so loudly through speakers I could feel it vibrating in my chest. *Boom-babba boom-babba boom-babba!!!* There wasn't another male customer in the place. Except for two male barbers, the place was full of women—all staring at me.

I was wearing a gray suit and had, in comparison to everyone else in the place, closely cropped, neatly combed hair. They looked as if they had stepped off the pages of a fashion magazine. They were wearing skintight, black leather pants, high-heeled shoes, and neon orange blouses. They did things with their hair I had never done with mine, shaving it in some spots and spiking it in others. They walked in an affected manner and were overbearingly friendly.

I was momentarily stunned. I have rarely felt more out of place in my life. I looked like a penguin in a flock of flamingoes. I turned on my heels to leave and nearly flattened a receptionist.

"Do you have an appointment?" she asked with eager anticipation.

"Uh, yes," I admitted, my ears radiating my embarrassment. "My name is Max Anders."

"Oh, yes, Mr. Anders. I've scheduled you with Delilah (not her real name. I don't remember her real name). She's just finishing up with someone and will be ready for you in just a moment. Why don't you go over to Cleopatra (not her real name either, but these names help you get the feel of the place). She'll shampoo your hair and get you ready for Delilah."

I looked like a penguin in a flock of flamingoes.

The shop was one big, open room, with a couple dozen hair-washing and cutting booths around the perimeter that opened to the middle. I walked across the open center area to Cleopatra's booth. Dozens of pairs of eyes burned into the back of my head. I stared at my shoes.

Cleopatra put me in a tilt-back chair that deposited my head in a sink behind me and began washing my hair. I can't explain how she did it, but she seemed to be sudsing my head in an unusually friendly manner. Then she rinsed, sudsed again, rinsed, conditioned, and rinsed. Delilah still wasn't ready for me, so Cleopatra began to massage my head. She asked me if it felt good. It felt wonderful, but I hated to admit it.

We made small talk. I probably seemed relaxed on the outside, but inside I was screaming, "Let me out of here!" My toes curled under in my shoes. My fingernails dug into my kneecaps. My jaw muscles tensed convulsively. *What am I doing here? What if someone in my church sees me here with Cleopatra, acting like we are long-lost friends? What if someone thinks I came here knowing what kind of place it was?* I could see the headlines in the paper: *"Local Pastor Gets Haircut at Delilah's Den!"* Subheading: *"Under Pressure, Admits Enjoying Scalp Massage!"*

Finally Delilah was ready for me. I got out of Cleopatra's chair and again slunk across the room, my eyes darting nervously. I crawled reluctantly into Delilah's chair, and in response to her questions, I shouted how I wanted my hair cut. (We both had to talk very loudly to be heard over the deafening *Boom-babba, boom-babba.*) As Delilah began to cut, the music stopped

---

abruptly, just in time to allow her to shout into the tomblike silence, "And what do you do, Mr. Anders?" Every head in the place turned in my direction. The suddenness of the music stopping, the volume of Delilah's ill-timed question, and the clear cultural difference between me and every other person in the place gave them all an intense interest in my answer. They all strained to hear.

I cracked.

I felt so out of place, so conspicuous, so embarrassed about being a pastor that I did the only thing that occurred to me at the moment. I lied!

"I'm a landscape architect," I heard myself croak. The answer seemed to satisfy everyone. Their heads turned back, the music started up again, and their world returned to normal. Mine collapsed. *Landscape architect? Why did I say that? I don't know a thing about landscaping. Why didn't I tell her I was a pastor? Because I'm a chicken. I'm an overeducated, undercommitted, gutless wonder!* I admitted to myself.

Back in my office, I slumped in my chair like someone who had just lost everything. I was overwhelmed with remorse. I laid my head on my desk and absorbed the crushing weight of my shame and guilt.

As the Holy Spirit drove back and forth over me like a steamroller over a hunk of human asphalt, I realized the pro-found conviction under which I was buried was not a result of having told a "white lie." It was because, out of fear and embar-rassment, I had publicly denied Jesus.

I had lied to save my own emotional skin, just as Peter had lied the night Jesus was betrayed. I now knew I would have done exactly what he did. I would have hidden in the shadows while Jesus was taken to the cross.

As I sat there, my head on my desk, my hands sprawled out in front of me, breathing laboriously into my desk pad, it slowly dawned on me what I had to do. I had confessed my sin to God. Now I had to call Delilah, confess my sin to her, and ask her to forgive me. It was the last thing in the world I wanted to do, but the Holy Spirit had me facedown on the sidewalk and wasn't letting me up.

When she came to the phone, I said, "When you asked me what I did for a living, I felt out of place and embarrassed, and I didn't tell you the truth. I told you I was a landscape architect. But I'm not. I'm the pastor of a local church. It was wrong for me to lie to you, and I would like to ask if you would forgive me."

Delilah didn't know what to say. She began to babble. "Oh, don't worry about that, Mr. Anders. Lots of people have second jobs. . . . Why, I didn't think a thing. . . . Heavens, it doesn't. . . . Don't give it a second thought."

"You don't understand," I returned. "I don't have a second job. I made it up because I was embarrassed to tell you I was a pastor. That was wrong of me, and it would mean a great deal if I could know you forgive me."

Holiness is not a matter of never sinning. If that were the case, holiness would be an unreachable goal for all of us.

This went on for a while, with me asking forgiveness and her talking a blue streak. One last time, I acknowledged my sin and asked if she would forgive me. When she finally realized I was not going to let her go until she said she forgave me, she said she forgave me. I thanked her and hung up the phone. The steamroller drove off of me, and I began to come back to life.

I am so grateful to the Lord for the power of His conviction, for His refusal to let me go until I had done the right thing. I am so glad He held me to the standard of His holiness.

Holiness is not a matter of never sinning. If that were the case, holiness would be an unreachable goal for all of us. Holiness is a matter of ready repentance. When the Holy Spirit, whose ministry it is to convict us of our sins, *does* convict us, and we readily repent, then we are capable of living a life of practical holiness.

What is the biblical mandate for holiness?
The mandate for holiness is found in 1 Peter 1:15-16: "As He

who called you is holy, you also be holy in all your conduct, because it is written, 'Be holy, for I am holy.'"

The holiness referred to here doesn't mean theoretical holiness that looks forward to our complete holiness in heaven. It means practical holiness *now!* Paul says "be holy *in your behavior!*" (emphasis added). God would be less than God if He called us to a lesser standard. But at the same time, knowing we cannot become sinlessly perfect while still on this earth, He has provided a way for us to live holy—though imperfect—lives by cultivating a spirit of ready repentance.

What is the relationship between repentance and holiness?
God's holiness leads us to repentance, which establishes us in holy living.

Walk with me through Isaiah 6:1-8, and we will see the relationship between repentance and holiness:

In the year that King Uzziah died, I saw the Lord sitting on a throne, high and lifted up, and the train of His robe filled the temple. Above it stood seraphim; each one had six wings: with two he covered his face, with two he covered his feet, and with two he flew. And one cried to another and said:

"Holy, holy, holy is the LORD of hosts;

The whole earth is full of His glory!"

And the posts of the door were shaken by the voice of him who cried out, and the house was filled with smoke. (vv. 1-4)

In this passage we see God is absolutely holy. He is so totally superior to us that there is only one response to His presence: to drop to our knees or fall on our faces.

So I said:
"Woe is me, for I am undone!
Because I am a man of unclean lips,
And I dwell in the midst of a people of unclean lips;
For my eyes have seen the King,

The LORD of hosts." (v. 5)

When Isaiah saw God's holiness, he felt a deep sense of his own sin, and he repented deeply.

> Then one of the seraphim flew to me, having in his hand a live coal which he had taken with the tongs from the altar. And he touched my mouth with it, and said:
>
> > "Behold, this has touched your lips;
> > Your iniquity is taken away,
> > And your sin purged."(vv. 6-7)

When Isaiah repented deeply, God forgave deeply, cleansing him with burning fire, a symbol of God's holiness.

> Also I heard the voice of the Lord, saying:
>
> > "Whom shall I send,
> > And who will go for Us?"
> > Then I said, "Here am I! Send me." (v. 8)

When Isaiah repented, he was usable by the Lord. Deep repentance produced deep forgiveness, which resulted in deep ministry to others.

Practical holiness is rooted in repentance. When we are called to holy living, we fear that God expects us never to sin again, and you and I know that is a hopeless expectation. And, if we know it's hopeless, God knows it's hopeless. However, the blood of Christ cleanses His children from all sin.

Practical holiness is rooted in repentance.

We must take holy living seriously, but we must also be ready to accept the grace of God when we sin. As we sharpen and cultivate our understanding of the holiness of God, we gain a clearer and clearer sense of our own unholiness. This drives us to deeper and deeper repentance, which makes us more and more usable by the Lord. Following the pattern in Isaiah 6, (1) the holiness of God spotlights our personal sin, (2) we repent of our personal sin, (3) the sin is forgiven and we are restored to fellowship, and (4) we are ready for service.

What final lesson can be learned about holiness?

We must take holy living seriously, but we must also take seriously God's grace and forgiveness when we sin.

After much research and thinking on the subject of holiness, I would offer these nine critical observations on holiness. (I gratefully acknowledge *Rediscovering Holiness*, by that giant of our times, James I. Packer, who significantly shaped my conclusions on the topic.)

1. To repent means, literally, to turn around. Once you were walking north, and now you turn around and walk south. When an attitude or value is involved, it means we abandon one attitude or value and adopt its opposite.

2. God's agenda for the rest of our lives on earth is our growth into greater holiness. The God into whose hands we have placed ourselves is in the holiness business. Part of the answer to the recurring question we so often ask— "Why is this happening to me?"—is that God is using a painful experience to build into us Christlike virtue and holiness.

3. We're not cleansed from the effects of sin without pain. For Isaiah, it was the touch of a hot coal on his lips. The *Delilah's Den* experience, while it has its humorous side, was a deeply painful experience for me. All sin, seen accurately as having nailed Jesus to the cross, is painful when God helps us see it the way He does.
   I believe if I had been the only person on earth who ever sinned, Christ would have died for me. I also believe if I had only sinned once (I wish!), He would have died for me for that one sin. Therefore, I can look at any given sin I have committed and rightfully say, "That sin drove the nails through Jesus' hands."

---

4. The great task of holiness is to grow up by growing down. Christians become greater by getting smaller. Pride blows us up like balloons, but grace punctures our conceit and lets the hot, proud air out of our system. We bow to events that rub our noses in the reality of our own weaknesses, and we look to God for strength to cope.[1]

5. We all fail at living a holy life. When we are tempted to think more highly of ourselves than we ought, we should remember the philosopher Montaigne's words: "If a person's inner thoughts were subjected to public scrutiny, there is not a person alive who would not deserve hanging ten times in his life." Just try to stop sinning. Try desperately not only to cease doing things you ought not to do, but to begin doing things you should do—being loving, patient, and kind at all times. Try desperately, and you will see how completely you will fail.
To pursue holiness means to pursue Jesus because the better we know Him, the more clearly we see how little like Him we really are. This leads us to deeper repentance, which leads to deeper forgiveness, which leads to greater usefulness by God and greater holiness.

6. As we grow spiritually, we begin to see how short we fall of Jesus' character. We learn we will never stop falling short of His character. As a result, those who are going forward into greater holiness will have the impression, from time to time, that they are going backward. They are not.[2]

7. To grow weaker is to grow stronger. To accept each day's trouble, pain, and failure as evidence of our weakness, our need for God's strength is key to our daily cultivation of holiness. When we stop relying on ourselves, our knowledge, our way with people, our way with words, or even worse, our ability to deceive, manipulate, or get our own way, then we begin to grow in holiness.

8. When we sin, it doesn't mean our salvation is jeopardized.

It just means our fellowship with God is broken. Just as when we sin against our spouse, it doesn't dissolve our marriage, but it dissolves our fellowship. With the relationship intact, we restore fellowship by repentance and forgiveness.

We can become like Christ.

Other chapters in this book deal with specific differences that will be made in our life as we progress into holiness. For now, I want to reiterate the most important point: Holiness this side of heaven does not mean never sinning. It means repenting readily when we do sin. As the apostle Paul wrote, "I . . . always strive to have a conscience without offense toward God and men" (Acts 24:16).

Pride blows us up like balloons, but grace punctures our conceit and lets the hot, proud air out of our system.

Whenever our conscience condemns us, we repent, ask forgiveness from God and others (if necessary), and provide restitution (if necessary). Then our conscience is cleared. We are blameless. If we initiate this process the minute we sin, we live a life of holiness, and we grow by the grace of God into the character image of Jesus.

Life-Check

1. Carve out half a day to pray and meditate before the Lord on the issues of repentance, forgiveness, and holiness. Read Isaiah 6:1-8 and 1 Peter 1:15-16. Ask the Holy Spirit to reveal to you anything in your life you need to repent of. Make a list. Then, one at a time, go through the list and repent. (Don't wait until you *feel* forgiven to accept God's forgiveness. Remember that repentance is an act of the will, not a function of the emotions.) If any restitution or asking

of forgiveness needs to be done, plan how to do this. Ask God to give you a clear conscience as a result of going through this process. If you feel you need help in going through this process, find someone who is spiritually mature, whose spiritual life you admire, and ask him or her to help you.

2. What causes you the most difficulty in your pursuit of holiness? Anger? Fear? Depression? Materialism? Sensuality? Covetousness? What do you think you could do to ensure you are making satisfactory progress in that area? List all the possibilities. Then prioritize them and begin to work on at least the first one.

3. What experience(s) have you had that interferes with your pursuit of holiness? This is sometimes related to one of your weaknesses. At other times it is related to the values you learned growing up or some difficult experiences you had as a child. Is there something else beyond what you did in number 2 that you might be able to do to increase your victory over that experience?

For Further Reflection

Scripture
Isaiah 6:1-8
Ephesians 4:24
Hebrews 12:5-11 (note verse 10)
1 Peter 1:15-16
Acts 24:16

Books
Rediscovering Holiness, James Packer
30 Days to Understanding How to Live as a Christian, Max Anders

3

The Law of Obedience:
Finding the Fullness of Joy

The shortest distance between you and the life
you want is total obedience to Christ.

If you keep My commandments, you will abide
in My love, just as I have kept My Father's
commandments and abide in His love. These
things I have spoken to you, that My joy may remain in
you, and that your joy may be full.
John 15:10-11

W hen I was in graduate school, I worked at a clinic that provided remedial therapy for children with mild learning disabilities. It was a rewarding experience as I saw many children, who were obviously bright but getting poor grades in school and often discipline problems, turn into good students.

We gave them assignments to do, and then we left the room to go into an adjoining room where we could watch the students through a two-way mirror. The students were told we would be behind the mirror, but they often had short attention spans and forgot we were there. They would goof off, disrupt others, and forget about their assignments.

When they drifted from their task, we reentered the room, reminding them we were watching, and got them refocused. We used this technique to help the children develop longer attention spans.

Sin always has a price, and the price is in direct proportion to the sin.

It was comical to see the children begin to lose concentration. They would look up from their work slightly glassy-eyed and begin to glance aimlessly around the room. Then they might look right at the mirror and wrinkle their nose, stick out their tongue, or straighten their hair. Often they pestered their neighbors. It amazed me that they didn't remember we were behind the mirror looking at them. So much time passed without their seeing us, and they got away with little things, so they forgot someone was behind the glass.

When we went back into the room, they snapped back to reality. With red faces and embarrassed grins, they resumed their work. Over time, as they finally "got it" that we were behind the mirror, most of the students were able to lengthen their concentration span considerably, which helped them do better in school.

Doesn't this remind you of our relationship with God? Life is lived in front of a two-way mirror. God can see us, but we can't see Him. There are things we know we should or shouldn't do, but God isn't in the room. We can't see Him, and over time we begin to think He isn't watching anymore. So we stick out our tongues at heaven or we walk around goofing off or disrupting our neighbors. All the time, God is watching.

Life would go so much better for us if we would only remember that God is behind the mirror. But we have spiritual learning disabilities. We have short spiritual attention spans. God must sometimes shake His head at our behavior. We're supposed to be manifesting the character and proclaiming the name of Jesus; instead we are looking into the mirror of this world, making funny faces.

What happens when we disobey God?
You cannot break the laws of God. You can only break yourself against His laws when you ignore or violate them.

We think we can break God's laws. We can't. We think we can ignore the truth. We can't. We think we can sidestep obedience to God without paying a price. We can't.

Sin always has a price, and the price is in direct proportion to the sin. Some sins have a greater consequence than others. The sin of laziness doesn't have as great a consequence as sexual promiscuity, for example. But there is always a price.

The price of disobedience comes in two forms. First, it comes in the natural cause-and-effect consequences of our actions. If we are mildly lazy, for example, we might miss out on a promotion at work that would have paid us more money. No thunderbolt came down out of the sky to strike us dead. But we paid a price anyway—a natural, cause-and-effect price.

On a more sober note, if we are sexually promiscuous, we may pay the consequence: sexually transmitted disease, AIDS, dreadful emotional problems, or an unwanted pregnancy. There is no thunderbolt out of heaven to zap us. It's just that people who are sexually promiscuous often get sick or mess up lives—theirs and others. It is part of the natural scheme of things. Galatians 6:7-8 says, "Do not be deceived, God is not mocked; for whatever a man sows, that he will also reap. For he who sows to his flesh will of the flesh reap corruption."

On the other hand there are times when God does bring direct judgment into the life of a person for sins committed. There is sometimes a thunderbolt, as it were, zapping us from heaven. We read in Hebrews 12:5-6: "My son, do not despise the chastening of the LORD, / Nor be discouraged when you are rebuked by Him; / For whom the LORD loves He chastens, / And scourges every son whom He receives." Perhaps we committed the perfect crime and cheated on a business deal, yet the deal mysteriously fell apart, and we lost our money. An accident? A coincidence? Maybe not. Maybe it was divine judgment as God chastened us to encourage our repentance.

From this we see that there is always a price to be paid for disobedience. Sometimes it is the natural consequence of our actions. Other times it is divine discipline, commensurate with the sin.

Why does God require obedience from us?
Everything God asks of us, He does so because He wants to give something good to us and/or keep some harm from us.

Like an athlete under a closely scrutinized training program, a musician in a carefully monitored practicing regimen, or a soldier involved in specialized preparation for guerrilla warfare, there is no wasted motion with God. Every action, every attitude, every rehearsal contributes to the ultimate goal. If we get lazy or careless or rebellious, it only delays the realization of His ultimate goal for us.

We read in Psalm 19:7-11:

> The law of the LORD is perfect, converting the soul;
> The testimony of the LORD is sure, making wise the simple;
> The statutes of the LORD are right, rejoicing the heart;

The commandment of the LORD is pure, enlightening the eyes;
The fear of the LORD is clean, enduring forever;
The judgments of the LORD are true and righteous altogether.
More to be desired are they than gold,
Yea, than much fine gold;
Sweeter also than honey and the honeycomb.
Moreover by them Your servant is warned,
And in keeping them there is great reward.

If these words are true—and of course they are—it would take an idiot to be willfully disobedient to the Lord. Yet, in spite of everything, we are disobedient! We forget God is behind the mirror. It is self-defeating. It is self-destructive. It is counter-productive. It keeps us from enjoying the very things we want from life. But we do it anyway.

What is the result of obedience?
The Scriptures promise joy for obedience.

On the other side of the ledger, we find the opposite conclusion: A person is blessed by God when he is obedient to Him. In John 15:10-11 we read,

If you keep My commandments, you will abide in My love, just as I have kept My Father's commandments and abide in His love. These things I have spoken to you, that My joy may remain in you, and that your joy may be full.

So we see in this passage that joy is a consequence of obedience.

Obedience is not nearly as hard if we become persuaded that it's not only for God's glory but also for our good.

Great blessings come to the person who is scrupulously obedient to the Scriptures, who doesn't ask, "How much can I get away with?" but rather, "How obedient can I be?"

If you believe obedience is the shortest distance between you and the life you want, you will obey. When you disobey, it is because there has been a breakdown of your faith. You don't believe the course of obedience will bring happiness. Or you don't believe a little disobedience will hurt all that much. Obedience is not nearly as hard if we become persuaded that it's not only for God's glory but also for our good.

<hr />

An obedient life has wonderful rewards.

I told a story in one of my previous books, *30 Days to Understanding the Bible*, that I think illustrates well the consequences of obedience and disobedience:

> I went to a professional dog show once and, in observing the relationship between man and dog, received instruction on the relation of God and man, and on meaning and purpose in life.
>
> The obedience trials, which took place within a large, square green of closely mowed grass, were particularly interesting. Several tests of obedience were displayed.
>
> 1. One at a time, the dogs had to start, stop, change directions, sit, stay, and return to their master, following a prescribed course that took them all over the lawn, without any verbal commands . . . only hand signals.
>
> 2. The dogs had to select, out of a pile of "dumbbells," one wooden dumbbell that their master had handled. The dumbbell was identical to all the others except for its identification number.
>
> 3. On command, the dogs had to jump back and forth over a high, solid wooden hurdle. Again, only hand signs were used.
>
> 4. The dogs were required to lie down in the center of the lawn, and upon being told to "stay" were required to remain there for a number of minutes while being totally ignored by their master, who was out of sight behind a canvas.

Two dogs in particular stood out. One was a large white German shepherd. He was an eager, grinning, tongue-lolling, fun-loving dog, but not fully trained. While enduring one of the early "sit-stay" commands, he spied a cottontail rabbit hopping at leisure around the back edge of the lawn. The large, well-muscled paragon of canine virtue began trembling like a white Jell-O statue, eyes riveted in utter absorption on this rodent treasure.

As though deliberately baiting him, the rabbit began cavorting playfully around the base of a mesquite bush, gamboling about in utter ecstasy under the inflamed scrutiny of the shepherd.

One final tantalizing hop was more than the white powder keg could endure, and, as though shot out of a cannon, the shepherd exploded in the direction of the rabbit. Both disappeared quickly into the bush, not to be seen in public again. While entertaining to watch, the dog was a failure, an embarrassment to its owner. Untrained, he did not yet attain to that marvel of harmony and communication that exists between skillful trainer and well-trained dog.

In contrast to the white German shepherd was a glorious, silky golden retriever. The retriever's excellence was as great as the shepherd's failure. Obedience to every command was instantaneous and perfect. Before, during, and after each command, the eyes of the golden were, rather than roaming the horizon for signs of life, fixed devotedly . . . no, adoringly, on the young girl who was his owner and trainer. After each drill the dog would return to her side, and with head up, tongue hanging out, panting, stare into her eyes for the next command.

After the dogs had gone through the trials, all the trainers and canines lined up for the awards. Fourth prize went to a springer spaniel, third to a German shepherd, second to a black lab. All during this time, the golden retriever sat obediently beside his master, looking up into her eyes.

Finally, first prize went to this marvelous dog and the girl who trained him. A ripple of applause washed through the audience, then crowd and contestants began to disperse. As they did, a marvelous thing happened. The girl wheeled to face her dog, squealed with delight, and began clapping her hands together excitedly. At this, the dog lunged up toward the girl's face in a desperate attempt to lick her on the mouth. She laughed and pushed him back. He tried again. She began running toward her car, laughing, clapping in unbridled joy, as her dog barked and jumped and circled around her all the way, sharing completely in her joy.

Chills played up and down my spine as I watched in undisguised admiration the joy, the intimacy, the trust, the devotion, and adoration that flowed between dog and girl.

The intelligence, athletic ability, courage, and personality latent within this dog was developed to a higher degree, and displayed more effectively, than any other dog I have ever seen. I thought, "This is the highest good to which I have ever seen canine life elevated." He was a marvel. A tribute to himself and his master. But everyone knew that the skill, intelligence, insight, patience, and personality of the owner were also on display. A lesser trainer could not have gotten so much from her charge. Glory to the dog! Glory to the owner!

Had that dog been left to his own world, he would have been just a dog, an ignorant slave of his basic instincts to run, eat, and bark.

There were surely times in the training process when the dog was unhappy. He wanted to quit, to run away. There were times when the owner wondered if he would ever learn. Before the training process was completed, the dog would gladly have been dismissed. But after the training process, the dog was happier and more fulfilled at its master's side than anywhere else in the world. The dog received that which it most wanted out of life from its relationship with its master.[1]

So are we golden retrievers, or are we white German shepherds? Are we out in the hinterlands chasing the cottontails of this world, or are we frolicking with our Master in the joy of obedience? The decision is ours: to obey and enjoy God or to face life on our own and suffer the seeming random blows of fate that always come outside the will of God.

Life-Check

1. Does it ever seem to you as though life is a two-way mirror, that God can see you, but you can't see God? Do you ever do things you know you shouldn't do because it doesn't seem like God is around? How do you think you can keep a clearer picture of the presence of God in your life?

2. Can you remember a time when you "broke" yourself against a law of God? That is, you violated a commandment of God's and then paid a terrible price for it? What insights does that experience give you for similar situations in the future?

3. Would you say you are more like the golden retriever or the German shepherd? What are some of the "cottontails" of this world that tempt you to flee in disobedience from the presence of God?

For Further Reflection

Scripture
John 15:10-11
Acts 5:27-29
Romans 6:17-18
2 Thessalonians 1:6-8
1 Peter 1:22
Galatians 6:7-8

Books
Loving God, Charles Colson
30 Days to Understanding How to Live as a Christian, Max Anders

4

The Law of Stewardship:
Taking Care of Important Matters

Stewards own nothing but manage the possessions and affairs of others.

It is required in stewards that one be found faithful.
1 Corinthians 4:2

*J*ack (not his real name) viewed everything he owned as belonging to God, considered everything he did as God's business, and lived his life to glorify God in all things, big or small. He was a superb handyman and was forever coming up with clever ways to fix things or make things better. He had a swing on his nostalgic front porch on Main Street in my hometown. But Jack didn't like pushing with his feet to keep the swing going. So he rigged a footrest that kept his feet up off the floor, and he tied a rope to the porch column in front of him and just pulled on the rope when he wanted to swing. It was ingenious and very comfortable.

Jack was swinging with his wife, Wanda (not her real name), one pleasant summer evening when the screws that held the swing to the ceiling of the porch suddenly pulled out. The swing dropped like a bomb to the floor, then like the next tick of a clock, the footrest tipped the swing over backward, leaving Jack and Wanda lying on their backs on the floor, their four legs sticking up in the air.

Jack's most flamboyant escapade occurred when he was mowing the lawn at their lovely piece of property on a remote section of the Tippecanoe River. Jack kept everything landscaped and manicured like a golf course. The lush lawn grew right up to the edge of the riverbank, which dropped off sharply to the river thirty feet below. The bank was unchanged from the days the Indians lived there—just trees, rocks, and underbrush.

One Saturday when Jack was cutting the grass along the bank, he got too close. The right front wheel of the riding mower dropped off the edge, and gravity, like a giant unseen hand, yanked the mower down the riverbank with astonishing speed. Crashing through underbrush, ricocheting off rocks, and bouncing over tree roots, the lawn mower, like a living thing, zig-zagged its way down the thirty-foot embankment without hitting a tree as Jack hung on like a bull rider. When it got to the river's edge, the mower dug into the ground, flipping the back over the front and landing upside down in the river, killing the engine. At the height of the mower's arc into the water, Jack launched himself into the air, diving into the river with the grace and beauty of an Olympic athlete.

Wanda was close by when all this happened and ran over to the riverbank. In her concern for Jack she wasn't watching where she was going, and she inadvertently slipped off the edge of the bank and slid all the way to the bottom, bouncing like a child sliding down the stair steps.

When she finally came to rest at the river's edge, Jack was standing in the waist-deep water just a few feet away beside the silent, upside-down lawn mower. Both Jack and Wanda were unhurt. Eyes wide, Wanda gasped, "Jack, what are we going to do?"

Jack replied, "Well, Wanda, I don't know. I've never done this before."

We have nothing of our own. Everything we have belongs to God and is to be managed according to His priorities.

While Jack had some bad luck, as shown in these examples, I will never forget the common thread running through them. Jack was tending to his priorities. He was fulfilling the requisites of a good steward, using his time, talents, and treasures God had given to him. He was utterly faithful in everything. He was efficient in his business, precise in his daily schedule. He kept his house, lawn, and car spotless and still had time to help others and to enjoy his family, friends, and Lord. Others might have different priorities from Jack, but few would be better stewards.

Of what resources are we stewards?

We are stewards of the time, talents, and treasures God has given us.

A steward is someone who administers the possessions and affairs of another. Properly seen, we have nothing of our own. Everything we have belongs to God and is to be managed according to His priorities (Rom. 11:35-36).

Everyone has been given the same set of resources: time, talent, and treasures. We don't all have the same measure or degree, but we all have some. So we are each to use our time as the Lord wants us to, our talent as the Lord wants us to, and our treasure as the Lord wants us to. That is the essence of being a steward.

Jesus taught in Matthew 25:14-30 that we are all responsible to use wisely what God has entrusted to us. The apostle Paul wrote in 1 Corinthians 6:19-20, "Or do you not know that your body is the temple of the Holy Spirit who is in you, whom you have from God, and you are not your own? For you were bought at a price; therefore glorify God in your body."

Nothing we have, not even our bodies, is our own. Everything we have belongs to God, and we are to use it in a way that glorifies Him.

Time: We all have bad "time days." I heard a story about a man whose secretary called him one day and asked who was in his office with him. He said, "It's me. I'm beside myself." Shortly after that he got his tie caught in his fax machine and ended up in Los Angeles. Then he got in his rental car and drove off in all directions!

The time pressures get so great and our world moves so fast, that managing our time according to *our* priorities seems almost hopeless. Yet nothing in the Bible has changed. We are still to manage our time according to the *Lord's* priorities.

We each have an equal amount of time: twenty-four hours a day. In the Scriptures, we read concerning time:

- See then that you walk circumspectly, not as fools but as wise, redeeming the time, because the days are evil. (Eph. 5:15-16)
- Walk in wisdom toward those who are outside, redeeming the time. (Col. 4:5)
- LORD, make me to know my end, / And what is the measure

of my days, / That I may know how frail I am. (Ps. 39:4)

- So teach us to number our days, / That we may gain a heart of wisdom. (Ps. 90:12)

It matters to God how we use our time. Our affairs are His affairs. It doesn't mean we are slaves to unpleasant obligations. Even Jesus rested and went to places apparently for enjoyment. But there is a time to play and a time to work. We are not to confuse the two.

Here are some suggestions on being a better steward of time:

1. *Reduce your earthly commitments.* If necessary, pull out of some of the things you are involved in. If you are overcommitted, accept that reality, and find appropriate ways to change it.

2. *Learn to say no to good things.* I don't know of anyone who is too busy doing *bad* things. Everyone is too busy doing good things, but too many good things add up to a bad thing. And the only way to correct the extreme busyness is to begin saying no to some good things.

3. *Write out your life's priorities.* Then decide which things you *will* do and which ones you *won't* do, based on your *priorities*.

4. *Schedule your time—your days, weeks, and months.* It is not out of line to plan out your year if that's helpful. Know how you're going to use your time, and use it that way. (If you have three kids in Little League, karate, and ballet, I can hear you laughing. I know, I know. There will be complications, but you will be better off trying and failing than not trying at all.)

5. *Pray over your schedule.* Be comfortable that you are using your time wisely, and then ask God's blessing on your schedule.

6. *Kick the TV habit.* Don't "brain out" on television, life's great schedule buster, or allow it to consume large chunks of your time. Watch according to your priorities, and then

make a conscious decision to turn the tube off immediately at the completion of your program.

7. *Tithe your time.* If it is true that God wants each of us to worship Him, pray to Him, read His Word, reflect on His truth, have quality time with our family, etc., then He will give us enough time to do everything else He wants done. We must learn what He wants us to do and not to do.

Talent: Each of us is good at something. Each of us has been gifted by God in some way (Gal. 6:10). And all talents require development and management if they are to be their best. Our talents are to be used for God. We may be a wonderful singer or a great artist. Those talents cannot be used in the world without consideration for the Lord. Everything we have and everything we are must come under the lordship of Jesus.

It matters to God how we use our time. Our affairs are His affairs.

We may have a talent for baking, or making people feel comfortable in our home, or working with numbers. It doesn't matter what our talent is. We must ask the Lord how He wants us to use it for His glory.

Treasure: Mark Twain was attending a meeting where a missionary had been invited to speak. Twain was deeply impressed. Later, he said:

> The preacher's voice was beautiful. He told us about the sufferings of the natives, and he pleaded for help with such moving simplicity that I mentally doubled the fifty cents I had intended to put in the plate. He described the pitiful misery of those savages so vividly that the dollar I had in mind gradually rose to five. Then that preacher continued, and I felt that all the cash I had carried on me would be insufficient, and I decided to write a large check. Then he went on and I abandoned the idea of the check. And he went on, and I got back to five dollars. And he went on, and I got back to four, two, one. And still he went on. And when the plate came around, I took ten cents out of it.

That is *not* the perspective we are to have on our money! We are to view it as God's and be willing to give of our finances to help advance the spread of the gospel, regardless of how long a preacher preaches. Obviously, we need money to put food in our stomachs, clothes on our backs, and a roof over our heads. God doesn't expect us to give all our money away. But we are to give as generously as we can and still maintain our God-given responsibilities (2 Cor. 8:13-14). Ten percent is an amount commonly given by Christians, but because of circumstances, a Christian might give more or less. The key is to pray, to ask God for guidance on what you should give, and to be at peace with the amount.

What are our responsibilities?
Each person has five primary areas of responsibility: personal, family, church, work, and society.

Here are some examples of these responsibilities.

1. *personal:* spiritual life, health, talents, intellectual growth, personal growth, finances, hobbies

2. *family:* parents, siblings, spouse, children, extended family

3. *church:* spiritual gifts, evangelism, financial support, fellowship

4. *work:* personal responsibilities, boss, coworkers, clients, general public, vocational growth

5. *society:* voting, being a good citizen, being a good neighbor, helping the disadvantaged

We are to direct our time, talents, and treasures into these areas of responsibility according to scriptural principles and the leading of God. How this occurs will be different for each person, and this can be tricky. Sometimes we feel like the ship that was carrying a cargo of yo-yos and got caught in a terrible storm off the coast of California. It sank forty-two times! When we try to keep everything afloat, we may sink about forty-two times. But we keep working at it, praying about it, and getting better at being good stewards in the areas of our responsibility.

With God's help you can be a good steward.

When it comes to being a steward of our time, talents, and treasures in the five key areas (personal, family, church, work, society), many of us may feel like a man one of my former students told me about (he swore this was a true story). My ex-student was working in a chicken-processing plant many years ago. The chickens were terminated (I can't think of a better word), dipped in scalding water, and placed on a conveyer belt. The belt deposited the chickens into a gizmo at the end that had a million rubber fingers whirling madly on the top, bottom, left, and right, with only a small hole in the middle for the chicken to pass through. The chickens came out the other side without a feather on them.

Life may never be simple or easy, but we can almost always make things better than they are.

One of the plant employees was profoundly obnoxious and spent a great deal of his time harassing the other workers as well as the boss. The boss was a quiet man who rarely said anything. One day, though, the man's behavior was particularly annoying, and the boss reached his limit. He picked the offender up and threw him onto the conveyer belt, which transported the man through the whirling gizmo. My student said he came out the other side beet-red and without a stitch of clothes on!

For many of us, that is a parable of life. We feel as though someone has picked us up and thrown us onto the conveyer belt of life, which has taken us through a whirling gizmo that includes our children, jobs, the house, the car, the doctor, dentist, family, neighbors, and church. We end up on the other side, beet-red, without another thing to give to the world. We're wasted.

The only answer is to get control, by the grace of God, and to try not to overextend ourselves. This is hard. We may need professional help. I have found time and money management books, seminars, and counselors invaluable. Life may never be simple or easy, but we can almost always make things better than they are.

Life-Check

1. Do you know what your life priorities are? Do you use your time according to your life priorities? If you don't, set aside the time necessary to establish your priorities and begin to use your time accordingly. (Stephen Covey's book *The 7 Habits of Highly Effective People* is an excellent resource for doing this.)

2. What are your strongest talents, gifts, or abilities? Are you using them according to the Lord's priorities? Is there anything you ought to begin doing or stop doing in order to use your abilities properly?

3. Do you have your finances under control? Do you support a local church and other worthy causes with your money? Do you think you are using your money the way the Lord would if He had it? What changes do you think you might need to make? If necessary, are you willing to make them?

For Further Reflection

Scripture

Luke 16:1-13
Romans 14:7-8
1 Corinthians 4:1-2
1 Corinthians 6:19-20
2 Corinthians 8:13-14
Galatians 6:10
Romans 11:35-36
Matthew 25:14-30
Colossians 4:5
Psalm 39:5
Psalm 90:12
Ephesians 5:15-16

Books

The 7 Habits of Highly Effective People, Stephen Covey
How to Manage Your Money, Larry Burkett
The Financial Planning Notebook, Larry Burkett

5

The Law of Servanthood:
Looking Out for the Other Guy

We were created by God to serve each other.

For even the Son of Man did not come to be served,
but to serve, and to give His life a ransom for many.
Mark 10:45

*S*erving others is not a popular idea these days. American culture is more concerned about getting others to serve us. Yet a spirit of servanthood is critical to a satisfying social experience. The Amish people provide a heartwarming example of this principle. My family comes from the rich farming country of north central Indiana, where corn grows tall, green, and thick as a full head of hair. A fair number of Amish live in the area, and I remember the Amish boys in my school in flat straw hats, plain blue shirts, and denim trousers held up by suspenders. The Amish girls wore plain, solid-color dresses and little white bonnets you could see through.

When I was young, I thought Amish children were odd. They had unusual haircuts and wore unusual clothes and tended to keep to themselves a bit. Even so, I remember that Rebecca Miller (not her real name) was one of the smartest girls in our class, and Harry Yoder (not his real name) was one of the best athletes in the whole school. Then when Rebecca and Harry turned sixteen, they disappeared. I never saw them again because the Amish attended public school only as long as the law mandated it—until their sixteenth birthday.

Today I don't think the Amish are so odd. In fact, the older I get, the more admiration I have for them. Their culture is not perfect; no culture is. They have jealousy, gossip, and pride just as all cultures do. But they are not plagued by alcoholism, drug abuse, teenage pregnancies, marital infidelity, bankruptcies, divorce, depression, suicide, crime, or many of the other plagues of our modern culture. For the most part they are peace-loving, loyal, hardworking, religious, and happy people. We could all learn from them.

There are many distinctive things about the Amish way of life, and one of the most notable is the way they look out for one another. Nearly everyone has heard of Amish barn raisings in which an entire community will gather to erect, often in one day, a barn that one of the families needs. They know that if they help build a barn for their friends when they need one, their friends will build a barn for them if they should ever need one.

It is an impressive sight. Scores of men gather at the building site with precut beams and lumber and under the direction of experienced builders, they erect the post-and-beam frame on a foundation that has already been laid. Then the roof and siding go on in a hurry. Meanwhile, the women cook enough food to cover row after row of tables while children gawk at the proceedings or go off to play.

In all cases, those in power are to use their position for the good and welfare of those under their authority.

It is a kind of social security—a caring, sensitive, and wise social security. The Amish are a band of people who have agreed to look out for the welfare of the others, knowing that the others will look out for them.

The Amish manifest many characteristics that the church of Jesus Christ at large is supposed to manifest but often doesn't. They live as servants to one another. And when everyone lives as a servant to others, everyone's needs are met in a context of unity and harmony. When we spend our time looking out for number one, only the lucky get their needs met, and that is in a context of selfishness and alienation.

How different this perspective is from the American outlook. From our Revolutionary War fathers to our Civil War fathers to our pioneer fathers, we're used to standing straight, sitting tall in the saddle, and being beholden to no one. Hard work, rugged individualism, and fierce pride went a long way toward building this nation. But it has a downside: Many of us barely know how to live in fellowship and harmony with others. The characteristics that foster fellowship and harmony—serving others, admitting we're wrong and apologizing, giving the benefit of a doubt, walking the extra mile, turning the other cheek, giving time and money to others when you may not ever get it back—

are often seen as evidence of weakness or stupidity. As a result, we often live as a collection of human islands, in proximity to others but not in communion. It makes for lonely people and a difficult life.

What does the Bible teach about servanthood?
The Bible teaches that we are to live as servants to one another, especially within the church.

We read in Mark 10 that two of Jesus' disciples, James and John, asked to be given positions of honor when Jesus established His kingdom. The other ten disciples got bent out of shape about it, so Jesus called them together to solve the dispute:

> You know that those who are considered rulers over the Gentiles lord it over them, and their great ones exercise authority over them. Yet it shall not be so among you; but whoever desires to become great among you shall be your servant. And whoever of you desires to be first shall be slave of all. For even the Son of Man did not come to be served, but to serve, and to give His life a ransom for many. (Mark 10:42-45)

Not only did Jesus teach this, He lived it. He washed His own follower's grimy feet, a chore normally reserved for a slave (John 13:5). This was a revolutionary message in a culture that was very class conscious. Power, position, and privilege were keenly sought after everywhere, among both Jews and Romans. Jesus was definitely swimming upstream.

Later, the apostles also taught the principles of servanthood. In Philippians 2:1-4 Paul wrote one of the most eloquent statements ever made on the heart of a servant:

> Therefore if there is any consolation in Christ, if any comfort of love, if any fellowship of the Spirit, if any affection and mercy, fulfill my joy by being like-minded, having the same love, being of one accord, of one mind. Let nothing be done through selfish ambition or conceit, but in lowliness of mind let each esteem others better than himself. Let each of you look out not only for his own interests, but also for the interests of others.

Even those in authority are to serve those under them. All authority is to be used benevolently, for the good of those under authority, whether it is husband/wife relationships (Eph. 5:22-31), parent/child relationships (Eph. 6:1-4), employer/employee relationships (Eph. 5:4-9), government/citizen relationships (1 Peter 2:13-14), or church/member relationships (1 Peter 5:1-4). In all cases those in power are to use their position for the good and welfare of those under their authority. That is the spirit of servant-leadership.

Chuck Colson, in his book *A Dangerous Grace*, wrote:

> Nothing distinguishes the kingdoms of man from the kingdom of God more than their diametrically opposed views of the exercise of power. One seeks to control people, the other to serve people; one promotes self, the other prostrates self; one seeks prestige and position, the other lifts up the lowly and despised. As citizens of the Kingdom today practice this view of power, they are setting an example for their neighbors by modeling servanthood.[1]

How do we demonstrate servanthood today?
We can demonstrate servanthood today by doing what we can to meet the needs of others.

Obviously, we cannot meet everyone's needs. Even Jesus admitted that the poor would always be with us. Even Jesus ate while others were hungry. If we gave away all our money, we would not make a dent in poverty, and our own families would starve. If we spent 100 percent of our time serving others, we would soon dry up. Jesus rested and enjoyed recreation too.

Nevertheless, we are to help others in need when it lies within our power to do so. There are many ways to do this. The following true stories offer some examples. (Names and circumstances have been changed to preserve anonymity.)

Susan and John were married under ordinary circumstances and began living an ordinary life. Their relationship was neither a blessing nor a curse. It was somewhere in the middle. As time passed they both began to change, but in opposite directions. Susan began to feel a stirring, a hunger in her heart for something more than this world was offering. John, on the other hand, began to "dull out." He worked too hard, watched too much television, and drank too much beer. He lost interest in most everything around him, including Susan.

> ## *We are to help others in need when it lies within our power to do so.*

The pain of the boredom and rejection in her marriage finally got to Susan, and she began to let herself go. An attractive woman, she gained a lot of weight, stopped caring about her appearance, began to nag and criticize John, quit cooking meals, and began spending a lot of time with other women who had similar marriages.

However, in the course of events Susan became a Christian, and while her fundamental desires changed, she stumbled a little in her approach. Now, instead of nagging John about not mowing the lawn, she nagged him about not going to church with her. Things got worse instead of better.

When she understood the Scriptures more clearly and learned her role was to respect her husband even if she did not respect his lifestyle, she made a fundamental change. Instead of trying to change John, she decided just to love him as best she could and give her life to Jesus as completely as any missionary or nun would. She gave up her expectations to get what she wanted out of *this* life, dedicated herself to serving Jesus, and put her hope in the next life.

She quit nagging John, lost weight, started taking better care of herself, quit running around all the time, began cooking again, and took on an air of peace about her that was new to John.

Obviously John noticed. He tested her severely. He reacted negatively to nearly everything she did. He questioned her motives about why she was looking better, criticized her new healthy ("Ptuhey!") cooking, and mercilessly ridiculed her about going to church.

But since Susan had not made those changes to change John but rather to serve Jesus, she stuck to her guns. Finally the weight of the change broke John. At first he simply quit attacking her. Then he began to be nice to her. Finally John himself became a Christian, and while the change in his life came more slowly than in Susan's, he did change, and their marriage became an example of spiritual unity.

Susan's attitude of servanthood was costly and painful for her. She had no guarantees that John would change. (Nor is there a guarantee that if another woman acts the way Susan did, her husband will change the way John did.) But Susan's desire was to serve Jesus by serving her husband. How her husband responded was not the determining issue in her faithfulness. The affirmation of God was. That is one way of being a servant in today's world.

Billy was a six-year-old terror. He made Dennis the Menace look like a choirboy. His primary goal in life appeared to be to make the life of his neighbor, Jim, miserable. Jim drove home one day to find his tomato plants stripped of all their fruit, which was scattered all over the yard. Another day Billy drove his big-wheel through the day lilies, flattening them as though a cow had laid on them. Once Billy turned on the water sprinkling system while Jim was working in the yard, soaking him.

Needless to say, all this got on Jim's nerves. When his own threats and intimidation tactics failed to achieve results, Jim hauled Billy to his mother. Billy's mother was understandably embarrassed and chagrined and tried to get Billy to mend his ways, all to no avail.

One day, after a two-week summer vacation, Jim and his wife pulled back into their driveway only to see Billy staring at them over the fence, looking as though he had spent the entire time plotting his next disaster. For some reason—perhaps the two-week respite—Jim saw Billy in a new light. The boy looked less like a pest and more like a vulnerable little kid. So when he got out of the car, Jim said, "Hi, Billy. How is your summer vacation going?"

Billy looked stunned.

"Are you going anywhere for vacation this summer?"

Cautiously, Billy told Jim of a summer camp that he would be attending in a few weeks, and of a brief visit to his grandparents' home in the next state. It was a short conversation, but there was something in Billy's expression that changed. There was interest there—an appeal for friendship. He smiled. Jim smiled. They chatted for a while, and Jim showed Billy some things he had gotten while on his vacation travels.

In the months that followed a friendship blossomed. Billy was no longer Jim's tormentor. He became a curious, generous, lovable next-door neighbor. The war was over.

Loving others even when they seem unlovable is another way we can serve.

Fred couldn't believe it. Through a series of unfortunate events he found himself out of a job, and then his family lost their home. Suddenly he was homeless! He had never thought it could happen to him. After all, he was hardworking, conscientious, and dependable.

With no place to turn, he and his family moved into a homeless shelter, which solved their immediate problem, but Fred was consumed with bitterness and humiliation. He was a stick of human dynamite with a short fuse. He got another job before long, but it would be months before he could save enough money to get his family back into a house. He complained bitterly and constantly.

Finally Fred realized that his attitude was affecting the happiness of his wife, his children, and everyone around him. He prayed for God's help to cope with his circumstances. His bitterness began to melt away, and he decided that while he was at the shelter he would try to help others deal with the humiliation and shame they were feeling. One day he spoke to a person who seemed to be struggling with a broken spirit. The conversation broke the ice, and the man grew less angry over the following weeks.

In the following months Fred talked to as many people as he

could, and if they let him, he prayed with them. The iciness that seemed to inhabit the shelter began to thaw as people became more friendly toward each other. Hope had begun to ease back into their lives.

To be a servant, we must give up our agenda to gain personal success and advancement at the expense of others.

Eventually Fred and his family were able to move out of the shelter, but Fred still went back to talk with the people, to help them adjust to the environment, and to help them get back on their feet.

Reflecting God's love in whatever circumstances we may find ourselves—still another way we can serve others.

We can serve others in the name of Christ.

I could tell story after story, but you get the picture. It isn't hard to understand. It's just hard to do. To be a servant, we must give up our agenda to gain personal success and advancement at the expense of others. Instead, we commit ourselves to the welfare of others and ask God to lead us as we give what we can to meet their needs.

It's a cold and lonely world when everyone looks out for himself. It is a warmer and friendlier one when we look out for each other—at home, at work, in our communities, and in our churches.

Jesus taught that we were to love our neighbor, and then He illustrated what that meant by telling the parable of the Good Samaritan. A Jewish man was traveling on a remote road and was ambushed by thieves. They beat him, took his possessions, and left him at the side of the road to die. Two religious leaders walked by and did not help him. But a Samaritan, who should have had a culturally induced hatred for a Jew, stopped and helped the man.

"This man," Jesus said, referring to the Samaritan, "showed love for his neighbor." As we follow Jesus' teaching, we fulfill the Law of Servanthood.

Life-Check

1. Why do you think more people don't have the values exemplified by the Amish? What prevents all of society from functioning that way? What prevents churches from functioning that way? Do you see a solution, at least within our churches?

2. How do you think the world would be different if all people in authority used their authority only for the welfare of those under them? In the relationships in which you have authority, do you consistently use your authority for the good of those under you? If you don't, why not?

3. Where do you think we should draw the line, not only in money, but in time and emotional energy, between helping others and meeting our own needs and the needs of those we are responsible for?

For Further Reflection

Scripture

Matthew 5-7
Mark 10:35-45
Philippians 2:1-11
John 13:5
Ephesians 6:1-9
1 Peter 2:13-14
1 Peter 5:1-4

Books

Improving Your Serve, Chuck Swindoll

6

The Law of Discipline:
The Slavery Required for Freedom

To be free to sail the seven seas, you must
make yourself a slave to the compass.

I discipline my body and bring it into subjection,
lest, when I have preached to others, I myself
should become disqualified.
1 Corinthians 9:27

I'll always remember how surprised I was the first time I ever took a swing at a golf ball. I fully expected to feel a solid thunk and watch the ball trace a great rooster tail in the sky as it flew hundreds of yards down the manicured fairway. My friends would gasp in admiration as they watched the ball surge eagerly into the bright summer sky. Instead, I didn't even hit the ball.

There was an angry whooshing sound as the club scared the ball but did it no damage. I felt a slight twinge in my lower back, which wasn't used to taking such a savage swing at something and not hitting it. Instead of gasps of admiration, there were tentative snorts of amusement as my friends tried to decide whether to reward me with sympathy or sarcasm. In a thinly disguised attempt to make it look as if I had taken a practice swing, I quickly swung several more times, deliberately trying to replicate my original attempt.

I approached the ball again, as one might approach a hornet's nest. *What in the world had happened? That ball was supposed to go flying. Why didn't it? What do I do next time to make sure it does?* I felt as though I was in the twilight zone with unknown laws of physics taking over my life.

It was an unpleasant situation. If I missed again, there would be no pretense. I tried not to think about it and attacked the ball once more. This time I hit it! However, instead of charging straight down the fairway, it sputtered off into the grass at a ninety-degree angle away from the fairway.

Well, the jig was up. I and my friends knew that I couldn't hit a golf ball. They compromised between sarcasm and sympathy. They sniggered derisively but never actually said anything. I picked up my ball, claimed my mulligan (a free swing off the tee—not in the rules book), and tried again. This time the ball dribbled pitifully down the fairway about a hundred feet (at least in the right direction this time), and I began a merciless assault on a dozen golf balls, alternating between losing them in the woods and cutting deep grins in their covers.

How could this happen to me? I had reasonable athletic skills. It looked so easy when I saw other people do it. If they could hit the ball down the fairway, why couldn't I? It was humiliating.

My golfing career was sporadic after that, climaxing in my first trophy at a golf tournament. I won the W.O.R.S.T. Trophy, which stood for **W**oods, **O**ut-of-bounds, **R**ough, **S**and Trap, and **T**rees, which is where I spent my time while everyone else was playing golf.

Only the disciplined ever get really good at anything.

The memory of my golfing experience faded, and several years ago I decided I wanted to learn how to play the piano. So I bought a book for adult learners and began to practice on a small electronic keyboard. It wasn't long before I realized that it was going to be much more difficult than I had ever imagined. After several months of practice, whenever I tried to play something it still sounded like a chimpanzee was loose on the keyboard. I eventually decided that I was willing to give whatever was in my power to learn to play the piano, *except* the amount of time required.

Sometime after that I determined that I wanted to learn to paint with watercolors. So for my birthday my wife gave me a six-week course of watercolor lessons at an adult education class at a nearby university. I was realistic, I thought. I didn't expect to be *good* when I started, but I didn't expect to be *pathetic*.

I was pathetic!

Everything I painted looked like a storm at sea. I tried to paint a rose. It looked like a storm at sea. I tried to paint a cardinal in a pine tree. It looked like a storm at sea. I tried to paint a sailboat at anchor. It looked like a storm at sea. My artistic skills had not improved noticeably since the first grade.

It wasn't until about then that I saw the connection among all these things and began to learn a gigantic lesson that has been reinforced countless times since: Almost everything is difficult to do well. From the simplest task, such as hitting a golf ball, to playing a musical instrument to flying a jet fighter plane, if someone is good at it, it is because he or she has worked hard at it. And to work long and hard at something requires discipline. So only the disciplined ever get really good at anything.

⟡

What are the costs and benefits of discipline?
You must limit yourself in one area to gain freedom in another.

Many people think discipline is limiting and restraining. And so it is. But it is also liberating and enabling. On the other hand, many people think total freedom is liberating and enabling. And so it is. But it is also limiting and restraining. All of life is a matter of freedom and bondage. If you choose one freedom, you get one corresponding bondage. If you choose a bondage, you get a corresponding freedom. For example, if you place yourself in bondage to brushing your teeth every day, you have the corresponding freedom of no cavities. If you exercise the freedom of not brushing your teeth, you have the corresponding bondage of cavities.

Have you ever looked at people who seemed to have everything? They are successful in their vocations, they have warm, loving families, and they have good friendships. They keep their lawns mowed and their flowers blooming, they have interesting hobbies, they're active in church, they seem to have it together spiritually, and they even seem to be physically fit. Chances are, if you get to know these people well, you will find out that they are well-disciplined.

On the other hand, if you see people who are failures at work, cannot sustain good relationships, have straggly lawns with a car rusting at the side of the house, don't have it together in any way, and are destroying their bodies with bad habits, chances are they are undisciplined.

I am by nature an undisciplined person. I would love the freedom to get up when I want, go to bed when I feel like it, and do whatever pleases me in between. But I learned fairly early in life that if I indulged myself in total freedom, I would never get any of the things I wanted out of life.

I wanted to play basketball in high school, but I wasn't good enough to do it without working at it. So I either had to start working hard during the off-seasons or give up my desire to play basketball. I wanted to go to college, but I didn't have enough money. So I had to either start working hard to earn the money or give up my desire for college. I wanted to have a rich relationship with my wife, but it didn't come naturally to me. So I had to work very hard at becoming a better husband or give up my desire to have a good marriage.

Now, people will occasionally remark to me how disciplined I seem, and in a way that's true. I am disciplined. But not naturally so. Rather, it is because I don't want to pay the price for being undisciplined. One of my seminary professors used to ask two fundamental questions of us over and over again: "What do you want out of life? Are you willing to pay the price?" Those were life-changing questions. They have guided me ever since.

How free you are in life depends on how disciplined you are willing to be.

Years ago, an Olympic gold-medalist in gymnastics from the United States, Mary Lou Retton, was asked if she ever thought about quitting before she got to the Olympics. "Oh, yes," she said. "Many times. But then, when I realized it would mean the death of my dreams, I always kept going." But, in order to get the gold medal, she had to give away her childhood. While all the other children were out playing and doing little girl things, Mary Lou was in the gym working. Not everyone, of course, is inclined to pay that high a price or has that level of commitment. But how free you are in life depends on how disciplined you are willing to be. Discipline is the key to getting what you want in life. It is the key to freedom.

———◆———

What does the Bible teach about discipline?
The Bible teaches that self-discipline is a virtue and a fruit of the Spirit we all ought to possess.

The Bible teaches the virtue of discipline. In Galatians 5: 22-23, the apostle Paul listed the fruit of the Holy Spirit, the characteristics the Holy Spirit gives to the person who lives in faithful obedience to Him. They are love, joy, peace, patience, kindness, goodness, faithfulness, gentleness, and *self-control.* Notice that *free-spiritedness* is not on the list. *Happy-go-lucky* isn't in there. *Fun-loving* didn't make it. Of course that doesn't mean it's wrong to be free-spirited, happy-go-lucky, or fun-loving. It isn't if you still do all the things the Holy Spirit wants you to do.

Let's look at some of the key passages in Scripture besides the Galatians passage that teach the virtue of discipline.

We are to discipline our body. "Do you not know that those who run in a race all run, but one receives the prize? Run in such a way that you may obtain it. And everyone who competes for the prize is temperate in all things. Now they do it to obtain a perishable crown, but we for an imperishable crown. Therefore I run thus: not with uncertainty. Thus I fight: not as one who beats the air. But I discipline my body and bring it into subjection, lest, when I have preached to others, I myself should become disqualified" (1 Cor. 9:24-27).

We are to discipline our spirit. "He who is slow to anger is better than the mighty, / And he who rules his spirit than he who takes a city" (Prov. 16:32).

We are to exercise "self-control." "Add to your faith virtue, to virtue knowledge, to knowledge self-control" (2 Peter 1:5-6).

Jesus taught that we should be faithful to use wisely the resources God gives us. He dismissed the one who didn't as a wicked and lazy servant (Matt. 25:26). So we see throughout the New Testament that self-discipline is a Christian virtue that needs to be part of our character.

Of course none of us is totally disciplined or totally undisciplined. And of course most of us are more disciplined in some areas than others. For example, we may be disciplined in our responsibilities at work but undisciplined in how we eat. Nevertheless, lack of discipline can be a devastating thing for many of us.

How do we develop more discipline?
We develop discipline by being faithful in small things and gradually going on to big things.

Those who are undisciplined find the task of developing more discipline a daunting thing to do. It seems impossible. You will never be more disciplined until you gain more self-control, but you cannot gain more self-control until you are more disciplined. However, being a fairly disciplined person by choice, not by nature, I can encourage you that the situation is not hopeless. There are several keys to developing greater discipline.

1. *Commit:* We must begin by committing our lives totally to the Lord and making the decision to be more disciplined.

2. *Pray:* God answers prayer, and prayer for the fruit of the Spirit is a prayer God will be pleased to answer. But be patient. He usually doesn't correct the problem overnight.

3. *Choose:* Decide what you think God wants for your life. Don't worry if you don't know for sure. Take your best shot at it, realizing you will refine the picture many, many times. The key is to begin. Be as specific as you know how to be. Because you have given yourself totally to God, it is reasonable to assume He will give you guidance through your gifts, interests, desires, etc. So to begin, you can roughly equate your desires in life and God's will for your life. If you ever come to the conclusion that something you want is not the will of God, you must drop it.

4. *Identify:* Establish your core values. They must line up with

Scripture, of course, and it's helpful to look through the Bible and identify the values you particularly want to govern your life. For example, if you're in business, you want to be sure you're honest. As a pastor, I adopted the value of integrity in financial and moral areas. You may want to have the value of honoring people or being true to your word.

Key passages to look at in determining the values you want to govern your life are the Beatitudes in Matthew 5: 3-11, as well as the passages concerning the fruits of the Spirit in Galatians 5:22-23, the characteristics of love in 1 Corinthians 13:4-7, and the qualifications of an elder in 1 Timothy 3:1-7.

5. *Prioritize:* Make sure you distinguish the non-negotiables in your life from those things that are merely strong desires. Focus on the non-negotiables. Then, if you're able, progress to fulfilling your strong desires. Be sure you're spending your time and energy and money on your life priorities.

When we have gained the independence that comes from mastering the core of our being, we then are able to achieve the goals and develop the relationships we long for. Stephen Covey writes, in *The 7 Habits of Highly Effective People,*

> The most important ingredient we put into any relationship is not what we say or what we do, but what we are. And if our words and our actions come from superficial human relations techniques rather than from our own inner core, others will sense that duplicity. We simply won't be able to create and sustain the foundation necessary for effective interdependence [with other people].
>
> So, the place to begin building any relationship is inside ourselves, our own character.[1]

Self-discipline is possible for anyone.

Though self-mastery is difficult for those who are not taught it or who don't come by it naturally, it can be developed. Even those who are undisciplined by nature and upbringing can improve significantly. You develop greater discipline the same way you develop stronger muscles: by exercising on a basic level and slowly but steadily increasing the level of difficulty. Discipline is a fruit of the Spirit, but the Spirit will not build it into our lives unless we are pursuing it.

> *You will never be more disciplined until you gain more self-control, but you cannot gain more self-control until you are more disciplined.*

When striving for greater discipline, start with one thing at a time. Perhaps you have trouble getting places on time. Set a goal of getting to church or work on time. Commit to that one goal and work on it until you are successful. Then set another goal and another one.

But be patient. It will take time. And be tenacious. You will slip often. When you do, get up again. If you make one change per month, that is twelve changes a year. In five years that is sixty changes. If you make sixty changes, you will be a different person.

You can be more disciplined. You can change. Begin now.

Life-Check

1. What do you want out of life? Are you willing to pay the price?

2. More specifically, what limitations do you currently have because you have taken the wrong freedoms? What freedoms do you currently have because you have taken the right limitations?

3. What freedoms do you not have that you would like to have? What limitations will you have to impose on yourself to get them?

4. What core values do you want to govern your life?

For Further Reflection

Scripture
Proverbs 16:32
1 Corinthians 9:24-25
Galatians 5:22-23
2 Peter 1:5-7

Books
The 7 Habits of Highly Effective People, Stephen Covey

7

The Law of Small Stuff:
Don't Let Life's Moles Build Mountains

If you let it, the small stuff in life will build up to become big stuff.

Therefore do not worry, saying, "What shall we eat?" or "What shall we drink?" or "What shall we wear?" For after all these things the Gentiles seek. For your heavenly Father knows that you need all these things. But seek first the kingdom of God and His righteousness, and all these things shall be added to you. Matthew 6:31-33

Why is it that the small things in life get to us? Like the night when my bed fell. I had flown to Chicago to conduct an all-day seminar in a church the next day. It was winter, and I felt like I was coming down with the flu. I was getting a sore throat and a mild fever. I hate colds and flu anyway, and to have to give an all-day seminar with the flu was something I did *not* want to do. I felt that my only hope was to take a bunch of vitamin C and get a lot of rest.

I checked into the hotel, ate an early dinner, and began getting ready for bed about 8:30. I wanted lights out by 9:00. Up by 7:00 would give me ten hours, and that just might help me avert a full-fledged case of the flu.

It was just about then I noticed all the noise out in the hall. Kids, thousands of them, rushing up and down the hallway like lemmings to the sea, making enough noise to raise the dead. *What in the world?* I wondered.

I stood in my doorway, glaring at them, hoping that my stern demeanor would reduce them to silence. I honestly don't think a one of them saw me. TVs blared from open doors; kids shouted from one end of the hall to the other. There was a small soccer game going on three doors down. The only thing comparable I have ever seen is Times Square on New Year's Eve.

They say when you have a brush with death, your whole life flashes in front of you. Well that night my whole evening flashed in front of me: I knew I would get no sleep! But I tried anyway. Better to light a candle than curse the darkness.

I called the manager. "Could you please send someone up to my floor to try to quiet these kids down?" I pleaded. "I'm not feeling well, and I have a big day tomorrow."

"Of course, Mr. Anders, we'll have somebody up there right away."

A half an hour later, lights-out time, it was noisier. I called the manager again.

"The noise is as bad as ever. Did you send anyone up?"

"Yes, Mr. Anders, but I'm afraid there are not enough adults to supervise the kids, and it apparently didn't do any good."

"Well, could you move me to another part of the hotel?"

This was a big hotel and maybe I could get away from the noise on another floor or wing.

Why is it that the small things in life get to us?

"I'm sorry, Mr. Anders, there is a regional YMCA swim meet here in Chicago this weekend, and all the kids are staying here. The entire hotel is booked with swimmers."

9:30 P.M. I was getting more desperate. *I shouldn't get this upset,* I thought to myself. *It's only working against me. I need to relax.* This was a nice hotel, and the shower was extra-large and enclosed in glass so you could turn on a nozzle and fill it with steam. It was a personal sauna. *I'll get in the sauna for a while,* I thought. *That will relax me.*

I steamed myself until, if I were broccoli, I would have been broccoli mush. I nearly lost the use of my legs. I groped my way back to bed, turned out the lights, and closed my eyes. Sixty seconds later, my eyes snapped open. I wasn't the least bit sleepy, in spite of the fact that I had nearly steamed myself into oblivion.

The bed had a vibrator on it. That would help me. I'd get good and relaxed. Maybe I'd even go to sleep while it was running. I put two quarters in just to be sure. All the time, the party was raging unabated outside my door. It's so hard to relax when you're uptight. It was 10:00 by now. An hour's sleep lost. All I could think about was suffering through a horrible day tomorrow because those inconsiderate little no-brain monsters were allowed to run amok while the adults were down in the restaurant or bar somewhere. Not very spiritual thoughts for someone who was going to spend the entire next day teaching the Bible.

My mental agitation plus the thorough cooking I had given myself earlier made the vibrator feel bad instead of good. It wasn't thirty seconds before I realized I had made a mistake. Oh how I wished I had only put in one quarter instead of two. I laid there trying to talk myself into relaxing. All the time I was vibrating like an electric razor. When my front teeth began to feel loose, I flung the covers back and got up. I stormed over to the chair and sat there for another ten minutes until the vibrator finally shut off. Ten-thirty P.M.

I was debating between suicide and homicide when it occurred to me (why hadn't I thought of this before?) I often sleep when the television is on. I turned on the TV and flipped channels looking for the best show to sleep by. In an instant I found it. A high school basketball game. Illinois was having its state championship game that night, and it was televised. Perfect. I sleep like a baby during sports events. I turned it on just loud enough to drown out the noise beyond my door but not loud enough to keep me from sleeping. Ah, finally I had hit on the answer. It was late but not a total disaster. I could still get eight hours of sleep, my absolute minimum.

As I lay there trying to drift off, I heard a half-crazed announcer scream, "It's fifty-one to fifty-two. It's fifty-three to fifty-two. It's fifty-four to fifty-three. It's fifty-five to . . .") My eyes bugged. I couldn't help it. Though I was living in Atlanta at the time, I was born and raised in Indiana, the Hoosier state. The Basketball State.

For reasons I will never understand, I somehow became "for" one of the teams. I had never heard of either team before. Soon I was shouting, "Go, Go, Go. Rebound! Defense! Shoot the ball!" In one of the most stunning victories I have ever witnessed, "my" team won by one point in the final second. It was exhilarating. There are few joys richer than a come-from-behind victory in basketball.

Eleven-thirty P.M. The euphoria left as quickly as it had come. There was still noise outside my door, but it had slackened to a dull roar. I fell backwards onto my bed, beside myself with frustration. I turned off the TV, turned out the lights, grabbed my pillow, and squeezed it around my ears. I turned over, and as I did, I bumped the headboard. It fell off the wall. I was beginning to get numb.

I put the headboard back on the wall, flopped back onto the

bed, and the bed collapsed. Mattress, box spring, and frame, all hit the floor. This was too much. *Am I on Candid Camera?* I wondered. *Where's the camera?* By now, I felt there was a national conspiracy to keep me from getting a good night's sleep. With zombielike mechanicalness, I put the bed back together and fell into it. Midnight. No noise outside. I was asleep in seconds.

The next morning, I got up at 7 A.M. The hotel was silent as a tomb. The little rascals would be able to sleep until noon. After I got ready to go down for breakfast, I had to fight the impulse to crank the television to its loudest volume, leave my door open, and sing "Oh, My Darlin' Clementine" at the top of my lungs, then bang on all the doors as I left.

Things go wrong, and they build up, and pretty soon, a bunch of little things have added up to one Big Thing!

The interesting thing is, I was not sick. I felt fine. My only problem was the guilt that I had as I drove to the church to teach people the Bible. I was remembering the murder I'd had in my heart for those kids the night before. I actually felt foolish.

The worst thing that could have happened to me was I could have been sick the next day. And while that would have been no picnic, neither would it have been a disaster.

How can we keep the little things from becoming big things?
We must consciously choose to follow Jesus' example in suffering.

Many things like that have happened to me. All kinds of things go wrong, and they build up, and pretty soon, a bunch of little things have added up to one Big Thing! Maybe they are tests to see if we will respond to them as Jesus would. When life throws its little things at us (for these were all little things), we need to take it as Jesus would. In 1 Peter 2:19-21 we read:

> For this is commendable, if because of conscience toward God one endures grief, suffering wrongfully. For what credit is it if, when you are beaten for your faults, you take it patiently? But when you do good and suffer, if you take it patiently, this is commendable before God. For to this you were called, because Christ also suffered for us, leaving us an example, that you should follow His steps.

What is accumulating in your life? Is it the endless drudgery of administrative details you have to take care of because there is no one to delegate it to? Is it the frustration of dealing with a teenager whom you don't understand and who doesn't seem to understand you? Is it the frustration of working your head off, and yet not making enough money to make ends meet? Maybe it's bad traffic you have to fight or a house that always needs repairs. These are comparatively little things. They are not cancer or a paralyzing accident or a child on drugs or a brother with AIDS.

All this is no more than Jesus put up with for our sakes when He came to earth. He bore it patiently. He is our example to bear our cross patiently.

But just how do we take it like Jesus would when the little problems of life mount up to become a big thing? Not being an expert on doing it right all the time, I would still like to offer seven observations.

1. *Differentiate between what is a big thing and what is a little thing.* Often we treat little things as big things and overestimate their importance. There aren't many big things in life. Life, death, righteousness, health, food, clothing, shelter, marriage, relationships. Most of the other things are little things. If we admit they are little things, they don't weigh so much or burden us so heavily.

2. *Take comfort in the fact that "all things work together for good to those who love God, to those who are the called according to His purpose" (Rom. 8:28).* Not everything that happens to us is good. But God will use everything for good. That's a truth that can encourage us.

3. *Learn to let go.* What does it really matter if I lose a little sleep? What does it matter if I get the flu? A hundred years from now, what difference will it make? When we put things into perspective, we can let go of the little things. It is only because we hold onto them that they begin to weigh us down.

4. *Realize everyone is plagued by little things.* You are not alone! It is *not* just you and me. *Everyone* is bugged by the small stuff. It happens all the time. It is a fact of life. If we accept that we are part of a great family of frustration, we can feel better.

5. *Decide you will not let the little things get you down.* Traffic in Atlanta, where I once lived, used to drive me wild. I drove about an hour to get to work, and it was stop and go much of the time. I'm sure my blood pressure was at an unsafe level while I was behind the wheel. I honked at people. I talked to them in a sub-Christian way. I arrived at work a bundle of nerves.

Not everything that happens to us is good.
But God will use everything for good.

Then I would sit down and try to write devotional material. On more than one morning, I thought to myself: *This is not right.* So I decided I would minister to people as I drove to work. I looked for opportunities to let people in front of me. I waved back at them as they waved thankfully to me. When people merged from an on-ramp, I was the good Samaritan and let them in.

I thought if I could appear overtly friendly on the road, I might encourage others to be the same. I might be the instigator of a great freeway revival in Atlanta! It transformed my driving habits.

6. *Give yourself to helping others endure their frustration and pain.* I

once read, "We ought always be kind to others, for they may be walking life's road wounded." I thought how many times I had been unkind to others, not because I wanted to be but because I was walking life's road wounded. It was a balm of healing when someone was kind to me. I decided I could be a balm of healing to others by being kind to them.

7. *Memorize Scripture in the areas of your weakness, and pray.* Ask God for help and strength in handling the little things. Get others to pray for you. Each time the devil tempted Jesus in Matthew chapter 4, Jesus quoted Scripture to him. If that was Jesus' strategy for handling frustration, how much more ought it to be ours? Get a friend to brainstorm with you on what practical measures might help remedy the situations that send you into orbit.

If you approach the problem with a good attitude, with prayer and Scripture, with creativity and maybe some help from friends, reduced blood pressure will be on the way!

What do we do when we stumble and fall?
We repent and get back up and start walking again.

Mind you, I don't execute perfectly. I said I had mastered the frustration of traffic, and yet one day I backslid. I was entering the freeway on my way home from a hard day at the church. It was Friday afternoon, I was extremely tired, very hungry, and had a slight headache.

As I accelerated to merge into traffic, my Suburban faltered. The driver of a BMW came flying up behind me, got within a foot of my bumper, and laid on the horn. Instantly I was livid. This jerk made me mad. He was driving way too fast, and he could have slowed down in plenty of time. He didn't have to ride my bumper the way he did, even though my car was going a bit slow. To top it off, he couldn't just toot his horn a few times; he had to lay on it!

This guy wanted to fight! In what (for a pastor) would qualify as a nearsighted rage (it wasn't quite a blind rage), I slowed way down to force him to pass me. When he did, I gunned the Suburban and got right up on Mr. BMW's bumper. My heart pounded with adrenaline. Acid poured into my stomach. My jaws clenched. I would see how he liked being tailgated by a vehicle twice his size and half his cost!

Now, there are several things wrong with this picture. First, it is sin to be so angry and respond the way I did. Second, it was dangerous. I could easily have caused a serious or fatal accident. Third, he might have been an armed psychopath and shot me. Fourth, it was expensive. A Suburban doesn't get good gas mileage when you drive it carefully. Accelerating the way I did probably cost me thirty dollars in gasoline. Finally (and this point hit me the hardest), *he might have attended my church!* People in our church drove BMWs.

I was consumed with shame and guilt. I began to envision what I would say to him after church the next Sunday when he told me about recognizing me on the freeway Friday. Given the shape I was in, like King David who followed adultery with murder, I would probably have lied, saying I was just wanting to be sure he saw me so I could say hello.

No, even when we take steps to keep the little things in life from piling up and becoming, by accumulation, a big thing, we won't execute perfectly. We will sin. When we do, we must repent and restore our fellowship with the Lord. Then we simply go back through the steps we took in the first place. Perfection can never be a reality in this life. But progress is something we all can achieve.

Respond properly to the "soup in your lap."

The story is told of a man who was interviewed by the vice president of personnel of a large corporation for a job that would bring a tremendous professional advancement as well as a major increase in salary. It was a delicate job, however—one that would require judgment, patience, wisdom, and extraordinary people skills.

After going through all the normal interview procedures, the vice president took the man out to dinner. Unbeknownst to the man, the vice president had paid the waiters to treat the man badly. They were totally incompetent! They took too long in waiting on them. They brought him the wrong order. They dumped soup in his lap. They charged too much.

Through the whole ordeal, the man being interviewed took everything in stride.

After the men left the restaurant the vice president said, "You have the job if you want it."

The man being interviewed was a little puzzled. It seemed like such an odd time to be offered a job.

The vice president's response was, "You obviously have all the professional skills and experience for the position. We knew that before you came. The last thing we needed to know was how you would deal with people under pressure. The meal tonight was a test. We paid those waiters to dump soup in your lap. If you had gotten angry or flustered or handled that situation poorly, you would not have gotten the job. You handled it well. The job is yours."

In life, when soup gets dumped in our lap, it isn't the soup that's the issue. It is how we respond to the soup. God is waiting to see. It's a test that, if we pass, we get promoted to greater maturity and usefulness to Him. And our blood pressure should be lower too!

Life-Check

1. What are some of the little things (such as traffic jams, the children, relatives) that consistently build up to become big things in your life?

2. What do you think you can do to begin to let go of the little things?

3. Do you have trouble dealing with guilt over your failures? How do you think you can keep the guilt from becoming part of the burden?

4. What are your ideas on how you can turn an irritation into an opportunity to minister?

For Further Reflection

Scripture

Matthew 6:31-33
1 Peter 2:19-21
Romans 8:28

Books

Strengthening Your Grip, Charles Swindoll
30 Days to Understanding How To Live as a Christian, Max Anders
How To Win Friends and Influence People, Dale Carnegie

8

The Law of the Mind:
Take the Garbage Out

We become what we think about.

A good man out of the good treasure of his heart
brings forth good; and an evil man out of the evil
treasure of his heart brings forth evil. For out of the
abundance of the heart his mouth speaks.
Luke 6:45

*T*he mind works in some pretty marvelous ways. I have a friend who has a near photographic memory. He used to perform in Shakespearean plays, and to memorize his part all he had to do was read through the play four or five times. Then not only did he have *his* part memorized, he had *everyone's* part memorized. He never seems to forget anything. Don't play *Trivial Pursuit* with him.

> ## If we put worthless, inaccurate, or faulty information into our minds, that is all we will get out of it.

This pales in comparison, however, to some other remarkable feats of memory. Renowned conductor Arturo Toscanini had a phenomenal memory and had memorized many complete musical scores—the huge books of music the conductor uses when he conducts a symphony orchestra. It has every note played by every musical instrument in the orchestra! Many of them resemble a phone book from a midsized city.

Once, just before a concert, a clarinetist came up to Toscanini and said that he would be unable to play as the E-natural key on his instrument was broken. Toscanini thought deeply for a moment and then announced, "It's all right; you don't have an E-natural tonight."

But as intriguing and intricate as the mind's capacity for memory is, even more powerful is its impact on our behavior. Proverbs 23:7 says, "For as he thinks in his heart, so is he." Luke 6:45 reads, "A good man out of the good treasure of his heart brings forth good; and an evil man out of the evil treasure of his heart brings forth evil. For out of the abundance of the heart his mouth speaks."

How does the mind work?
*The mind is occupied by what is put into it
and what it dwells upon.*

It is amazing how like a computer the mind is. A computer has a big memory bank where it stores whatever is put into it. The only thing you can get out of a computer is what you have put into it. There is an old computer term, GIGO, which stands for Garbage In/Garbage Out. It means if you put worthless, inaccurate, or faulty information into a computer, you will get worthless, inaccurate, or faulty information out of it.

The same is true of our minds. If we put worthless, inaccurate, or faulty information into our minds, that is all we will get out of it.

Unlike computers, however, the mind can create its own worthless, inaccurate, or faulty information. It doesn't have to be put in from the outside. Someone can tell us as a child that we are stupid, and we will water, fertilize, and nurture that seedling into a forest of negative thoughts and emotions.

That is why it is so critical that we exercise great care in what we allow into our mind and what we allow our mind to dwell on.

What are the trouble spots in our thought life?
*There are three big trouble spots in keeping our mind
focused on good things: the media, our friends, and our
inner thought life.*

The media today are, perhaps, the most powerful influence the mind has ever encountered. Television, movies, magazines, and music embed powerful images, thoughts, and values deeply, often permanently, within our minds. They either help us or hurt us. The care with which we guard what is allowed into our minds is crucial to our ability to know and do the will of God.

Our friends also have a dramatic impact on our values and behavior. The Bible says "Evil company corrupts good habits"

(1 Cor. 15:33). That is especially true for teenagers, but it is solidly true for the rest of us too. We tend to be like those with whom we choose to spend time. If our friends are not walking with God, it will tempt us not to walk with God. If our friends hinder our walk with God, we need to rethink our relationship with our friends, and either change our friends or change how we relate to them.

Finally, our inner thoughts can make what we allow into our minds either better or worse. Something bad can come into our mind, and we can overcome it by dwelling on the right thoughts. On the other hand, something good can come into our mind, and we can destroy it by dwelling on the wrong thoughts. In fact, our mind cannot really tell the difference between a real event and a vividly imagined event. Often our thought life can have a greater impact on us than outside input.

We must be aware of these three avenues for helping or hurting ourselves and use them for our good. Our ability to manage these resources will determine our destiny.

If we put lustful images and thoughts into our minds, we will get lustful thoughts out of it. If we put materialistic thoughts into our minds, we will get materialistic thoughts out of it. If we put prideful thoughts into our minds, we will get prideful thoughts out of it. Whether it is revenge, resentment, immorality, self-demeaning thoughts, defeatist attitudes, hopelessness, anger, or fear, if we put them in, and/or if we allow our minds to dwell on them, that is what we get back out.

The care with which we guard what is allowed into our minds is crucial to our ability to know and do the will of God.

On the other hand, if we put spiritual thoughts into our minds, peaceful thoughts, loving thoughts, encouraging thoughts, forgiving thoughts, then these are the things we will get out.

This balance is, of course, never all of one and none of the other. Even the most negative person will slip up and have a positive thought now and then. And even the most spiritual person will have a sinful thought. But what's the ratio? You cannot avoid all negative or sinful input. A billboard you see on the way to the airport, a TV commercial you see while you are trying to get a weather report, a swear word you hear while you are waiting at the checkout stand, are all things that the innate lure to sin within us (Romans 7 calls it the flesh) draws us to dwell upon. Also, the devil will see that we are never free of all negative and harmful input. So it must be offset by positive input.

What is the key to mastering the mind?

The key to mastering the mind is to guard carefully what we put into our minds, and what we allow our minds to dwell on.

First, we must choose the right values. Without the right values nothing else can be right. But even after the right values are chosen the battle is still far from won. We must guard tenaciously what we allow into our minds and what we allow our minds to dwell on. The apostle Paul wrote in Romans 12:1-2:

> I beseech you therefore, brethren, by the mercies of God, that you present your bodies a living sacrifice, holy, acceptable to God, which is your reasonable service. And do not be conformed to this world, but be transformed by the renewing of your mind, that you may prove what is that good and acceptable and perfect will of God.

We can gain more insight from this passage by thinking it through backwards. If we want to be living demonstrations of the fact that God's will is good and acceptable and perfect, we must be transformed. If we are to be transformed, we must have our minds renewed. If we are to have our minds renewed, we must present our bodies to God as a living sacrifice. So we start with a decision of total commitment to the Lord. Then we follow the Lord in renewing our mind.

How do we renew our mind? By stopping the inflow of hurtful input and increasing the flow of helpful input. For example, let's suppose that a Christian man has trouble with lustful thoughts. This problem may be traced to several factors. First, he watches network and cable television, including one of the premium movie channels, and regularly gets his eyes full of seductive images. He passes it off as innocent activity, as everyone else he knows also watches network and cable TV. Oh yes, some of the movies have steamy love scenes in them, but he is an adult, happily married, and he just ignores them because the rest of the movie is so good.

Second, he gets *Sports Illustrated* magazine, and its advertising often includes seductive images. And then there's the annual swimsuit issue, which would dilate the pupils of a saint. But again, he passes it off as innocent. It's part of our society now, and since we can't live in a cave, he rationalizes that he'll just read it and ignore the images. The articles are so good.

Finally, he has begun ogling the good-looking women at the office where he works and in the restaurants where he eats, and if the truth were to be known, he is even starting to let his eyes linger on women at church.

So why is our friend having trouble with lustful thoughts? Because he is allowing lustful data into his human computer— garbage in/garbage out. He wants the freedom to watch his television and movies, read his magazines, and look at the women with whom he comes into contact, but then shut it off. He doesn't really want the lustful thoughts, but the lustful thoughts come with the habits. The bondage to lustful thoughts comes with the freedom he is giving himself to input lustful data.

He is in a form of spiritual bondage, and while it has not taken over his life yet, it will if it is not stopped. The beginning point in gaining victory over his lustful thoughts is to stop the inflow of lustful data. Stop the television images, stop the magazine images, stop the girl-watching.

He must also input positive data that will offset and gradually give victory over the lustful tendencies. First, he must confess his actions as sin and repent of them. Second, he must present his body to God as a living sacrifice. Third, he must pursue the spiritual disciplines such as prayer, Bible reading, memorization, meditation, church attendance, and so on.

If he does these things, though, he may find the mental battle getting stronger instead of weaker. First, it's very hard to break deeply ingrained habits. We don't realize how hard until we try. Second, our adversary, the devil (1 Peter 5:8), may increase his efforts to tempt him and keep him mired in his bad habit. Therefore, he may need to join a men's group or a spiritual accountability group or develop a discipleship/mentor relationship to get the support and encouragement he needs. Lustful thoughts are no small thing. Countless thousands of Christian men are in bondage to these habits and think they can quit if they want to. But when they try, they discover they can't, and serious measures must sometimes be taken to break sin's hold.

We become what we think about.

Men caught in such bondage forfeit spiritual leadership at home and spiritual testimony at work and with their neighbors because of it. They forfeit the peace that comes with freedom in Christ over bondage to sin. They forfeit the joy of a life of integrity.

Here's another example. Let's say a Christian woman is having trouble with materialism. She grew up in a well-to-do home but is not able to enjoy the same standard of living as an adult. Her family's house, cars, furnishings, and "toys" are not as nice as those of her parents or friends, and it really bothers her. She overspends and regularly puts the family in serious credit crunches buying things they can't afford. She works long hours, even though she would rather stay home and be a mom to her kids, because it is the only way her family can come close to the standard of living she desires. She is sacrificing time with her kids, her husband, and her other priorities in life to make more money.

She subscribes to *Colonial Homes, Victoria,* and *Southern Living* magazines and feeds her desire for "things" by comparing her own possessions with the pictures she sees. When she visits someone else's home, she constantly compares their possessions with her own.

This desire for things gives rise to a growing resentment toward her husband for not making more money and being a better provider. This feeds her dissatisfaction and loss of romantic desire for the man she married. She feels trapped and unhappy.

This woman is in bondage to her passion for things. As long as she keeps reading those magazines with the same materialistic eye, as long as she keeps comparing herself with her friends, as long as she keeps measuring her life by the yardstick of material possessions, she will be miserable. She must shut off the flow of harmful data and increase the flow of helpful data, using the same strategies as the man with the problem of lustful thoughts.

Whether it is lust, materialism, anger, resentment, fear, anxiety, worry, or anything else, garbage in will yield garbage out. If we feed our minds with unhelpful information, we will make the wrong decisions, have the wrong values, trust the wrong things, and suffer badly for it all. We become what we think about.

<hr>

We must think right thoughts!

Most of this chapter has focused on the negative effects of wrong thoughts. But the positive effects of right thoughts are equally powerful. The apostle Paul wrote:

> Whatever things are true, whatever things are noble, whatever things are just, whatever things are pure, whatever things are lovely, whatever things are of good report, if there is any virtue and if there is anything praiseworthy—meditate on these things. The things which you learned and received and heard and saw in me, these do, and the God of peace will be with you. (Phil. 4:8-9)

Not only must we keep the bad stuff out, we must put the good stuff in. The mind is powerfully influenced by what we put into it and what we allow it to dwell upon.

Life-Check

1. On a scale of one to ten, how are you doing at guarding

what you let into your mind? What is the area of your greatest weakness?

2. On the same scale, how are you doing at guarding what you allow your mind to dwell on? What is the area of your greatest weakness?

3. Finally, on the same scale, how well do your friends encourage you by their own example to follow the Lord?

For Further Reflection

Scripture
Romans 12:1-2
2 Corinthians 10:5
Philippians 4:8-9
Luke 6:45
Proverbs 23:7

Book
Your Mind Matters, John R.W. Stott

9

The Law of the Tongue:
Words That Heal—Not Hurt

If we control the tongue,
we control the whole person.

Let no corrupt word proceed out of your
mouth, but what is good for necessary
edification, that it may impart
grace to the hearers.
Ephesians 4:29

*I*n high school, I was a B.M.O.C. A **B**ig **M**an **O**n **C**ampus. I was a varsity athlete in basketball and track, played in several school bands, was a class officer, had the lead in the school play, and was invited to all the parties the popular kids had. I was big stuff on the outside. On the inside I was insecure and easily threatened. I was an overachiever simply because I had no confidence whatsoever in my inherent worth as a human being. So I had to rely on my achievements to validate my worth as a member of the human race.

I would periodically do things to validate my status, to remind myself and others that I was, in fact, a B.M.O.C. Usually, these things were the actions of a J.E.R.K., which is often what I really was. But I didn't think so at the time, and neither, strangely enough, did the other popular kids.

One of my most disheartening forays into Jerk-dom began when a new girl moved to our small town. She was quiet and shy, though looking back on it even thirty years later, I remember her as a nice young lady. She had a pleasant countenance, was polite, courteous, and a good student. She wasn't beautiful, but neither was she unattractive.

But the ways of Jerks are difficult to fathom, and for some reason several of the popular guys singled her out for unwarranted attention. We used to talk about her within her hearing. Nothing ugly, just questions about where she came from, what she was like, and why she was so quiet. But especially because we did it within her hearing, it was terribly rude. She never said anything, never acknowledged our rudeness, and never lost the pleasant look on her face.

I remember one ball game where she was sitting in front of us, and we started blowing on the back of her head. Very slightly at first. We wanted her to reach back and feel the back of her head and wonder what was there. But she didn't. So we blew harder. She still didn't acknowledge our pestering. Finally we blew so hard we parted her hair down the back of her head. She did nothing. She never acknowledged our presence and never lost the pleasant look on her face.

We have, between our teeth, a tool that gives us the ability to encourage, exalt, and empower, or the ability to discourage, damage, and defeat.

To this day I don't fully understand why I did that. I was not a consciously mean kid. I think it had something to do with establishing my dominance over someone new, so I could reassure myself of my standing in the herd. But undeniably, it was the behavior of a pack animal.

When I think of it now, I reproach myself for my thoughtless actions. How I must have hurt her, and for no reason. Yet she was the picture of grace through it all. In reality, she was a B.W(oman).O.C. I was just a B.J(erk).O.C.! I don't know where she is today, but I wish I could talk to her and ask her to forgive me. I wish I could tell her how much I admire her for her graciousness.

Why do we use our tongue so carelessly? Why are we so insensitive to others? What motivates us? If I had to guess, I would speculate that most of our inhumanity to others is rooted in our own insecurities and sense of inadequacy. Like chickens fighting for a pecking order in the chicken coop, we fight each other for positions in the pecking order of humanity, often with words.

Someone once said, "Sticks and stones may break my bones, but words will never hurt me." Don't you believe it. Words can hurt and words can heal. Words can tear down; words can build up. Words can destroy and words can create.

We have, between our teeth, a tool that gives us the ability to encourage, exalt, and empower, or the ability to discourage, damage, and defeat.

If we had a physical weapon this powerful, it would have to

be licensed and registered with the authorities. Some people would not be permitted to carry it. Yet here we are, everyone armed with a weapon so powerful that lives hang in the balance when we use it. And many of us don't know how to use it well.

What does the Bible teach about the tongue?
The Bible teaches that the tongue is extremely powerful and commands us to use our tongue wisely.

God knows the power of the tongue. He gave it to us. And He instructed us on how to use it. The central passage in the Bible on the tongue is found in James 3:2-6:

> If anyone does not stumble in word, he is a perfect [mature] man, able also to bridle the whole body. Indeed, we put bits in horses' mouths that they may obey us, and we turn their whole body. Look also at ships: although they are so large and are driven by fierce winds, they are turned by a very small rudder wherever the pilot desires. Even so the tongue is a little member and boasts great things. See how great a forest a little fire kindles! And the tongue is a fire, a world of iniquity. The tongue is so set among our members that if defiles the whole body, and sets on fire the course of nature; and it is set on fire by hell.

Whew! Strong words. But true. And that's not the end of it. The Bible has more to say about our words. We saw in the last chapter on the Law of the Mind that "we become what we think about." The key passage on the Law of the Mind shows that what we've become is revealed by our tongue:

> A good man out of the good treasure of his heart brings forth good; and an evil man out of the evil treasure of his heart brings forth evil. For out of the abundance of the heart his mouth speaks. (Luke 6:45)

What comes out of our mouths originates in our hearts. The heart is the reservoir. Our words are merely the stream flowing out of it. How embarrassing! Everyone knows! They know our heart by listening to our words!

Changing our speech is not an easy task because it isn't merely our speech that needs changed. It's our heart. That's why James wrote that if we could control the tongue, we could control the entire body. Therefore, we must look honestly and accurately at our speech. Is it helpful speech or hurtful speech? No one speaks all of one and none of the other, but that must not keep us from being honest.

When we have a spirit of honesty and receptivity about our speech, we can look at the characteristics of good speech and bad speech with the goal of improving our own. If we use our tongue wisely and well, it will improve our relationships with other people and make our lives better. If we use our tongue unwisely and poorly, it will damage our relationships with other people and make our lives worse.

What are some ways our words can hurt?
We can hurt other people with lies, anger, gossip, or unclean speech.

Lies: I remember my first conscious, bold-faced lie. I was five years old, and I had taken six cents from my piggy bank (which I was forbidden to do without permission) to buy candy from the little grocery store in our tiny town. I plunked down my coins, chose the six pieces of penny candy that enticed me most, and lit out for the garden to hide. I was feeding rapturously on my illicit treasure when my brother found me and asked me where I got the money to buy the candy. I didn't think very far ahead at the age of five. I told him that Beverly (my oldest sister) had given it to me. I thought that would be the end of it. How was I to know the little snitch was going to go straight into the house and get to the bottom of this whole thing? He was strongly motivated by the fact that he hadn't gotten six cents to spend on candy.

Well, before I knew it The Snitch came trotting back to my hiding place in the garden and announced that Mom wanted to talk to me. I was caught. I confessed to the whole sordid affair and was punished by having to stand in the corner for an eternity.

Lying is wrong for several reasons. First, it is a sin against God.

Second, it is a sin against others. Third, it never pays in the long run. Sooner or later our lies catch up with us. People learn that we lie, and it ruins our reputation and our credibility. Proverbs 12:22 says, "Lying lips are an abomination to the LORD, / But those who deal truthfully are His delight."

Someone once said a great advantage of always telling the truth is that you never have to remember what you said.

Someone once said a great advantage of always telling the truth is that you never have to remember what you said.

When a Christian lies, he is hurting God's reputation, hurting his own reputation, destroying his relationships, and eroding his chances for success in life. Lying is hurtful speech.

Anger: A second common form of hurtful speech is an angry outburst. How easy, how natural it is for us to fly off the handle or say something unkind because of our anger.

A young boy once asked, "Dad, how do wars get started?"

His father replied, "Well, take the first World War. That got started when Germany invaded Belgium."

Immediately his wife interrupted him. "Tell the boy the truth. It began because somebody was murdered."

The husband stiffened and said, "Are you answering the question, or am I?"

The wife turned and left the room in a huff, slamming the door behind her. An uneasy silence settled over the room.

"Never mind, Dad," said the boy. "I think I know the answer to my question."

The Bible says that everyone should be "swift to hear, slow to speak, slow to wrath; for the wrath of man does not produce the righteousness of God" (James 1:19-20). How many times we get this turned exactly around, being slow to hear, quick to speak, and quick to get angry. But when we do, we sin. We don't achieve the righteousness of God.

Gossip: "Did you hear that Joe and Susan are having problems? It's terrible. Another woman, I think."

"Well, I'm not surprised. She's a compulsive perfectionist and drives me nuts, and I'm glad I'm not married to her. Not that Joe's right, of course."

"Of course. But look what it's doing to the kids. They're both teenagers now and wilder than March hares."

"Yes. It's too bad. They really need our prayers."

How many times conversations such as this take place in the name of "information for more enlightened prayer," when it's nothing more than gossip. Gossip is hard to avoid because it is so interesting, because when we share it we appear to be "in the know," and because our genuine interest and concern for others sometimes draw us into a deeper level of conversation about people than is appropriate. I do not consider myself a gossip, and I don't think others would either. And yet when I am totally honest with myself, it is amazing how easily I can get drawn into gossip if I drop my guard.

Spreading rumors is another form of gossip. How easy it is to pass along a piece of information we heard when we don't know for sure it's accurate. And how damaging, unkind, and hurtful this can be to another person—who may be completely innocent.

The Bible says it is wrong and sinful to be "wandering about from house to house, and not only idle but also gossips and busybodies, saying things which they ought not" (1 Tim. 5:13). Gossiping and rumor-spreading are other ways to speak hurtfully.

Unclean Speech: At one of the churches I pastored, a prominent lay-leader and I were talking at a social function. I asked him how his job was going. He had, what seemed to me from a distance, a rather exciting profession. His face clouded over, and he leaned over close to me and said in a confidential whisper, "Oh, it's a @%#* pain!" I couldn't believe it—not only that this man, who had a reputation in the church for spiritual maturity, would use such language, but also that he would lean over to me so other people couldn't hear and whisper swear words in my ear! Why did he think I would want to hear that language if it was unfit for the rest of the people in the room?

I have had similar experiences with people telling coarse or vulgar jokes. Why they thought I would want to hear such a joke is beyond me. I used to laugh hesitantly and shake my head a little so as not to embarrass the person. But I always felt guilty doing so because with my feeble laugh I felt I gave tacit approval to the story. Now I just look at the person. I don't laugh, and I don't say anything to let him off the hook. And I try not to appear holier-than-thou.

The Bible says, "Let no corrupt word proceed out of your mouth, but what is good for necessary edification, that it may impart grace to the hearers" (Eph. 4:29). Words of "edification" do not include cursing, swearing, or telling dirty jokes. Again, the apostle Paul wrote: "[Let] neither filthiness, nor foolish talking, nor coarse jesting" be part of your speech (Eph. 5:4). Rather, "Let your speech always be with grace, seasoned with salt, that you may know how you ought to answer each one" (Col. 4:6).

***

What are ways our words can help?
We can help others by using words of encouragement, by speaking the truth in love, by passing on good reports about others, and by being cheerful.

Encouragement: The power of encouragement is truly awesome. It can turn defeat into victory, sadness into joy, despair into hope. The most obvious form of encouragement is to recognize someone publicly. That's why recognition banquets are a good idea. A more subtle but possibly more powerful form of encouragement, however, is simply the everyday kind. Telling someone how much you appreciate his hard work. Recognizing the sacrifice someone made. Thanking someone for her thoughtfulness. Mark Twain once remarked that he could go for a whole month on the encouragement of one good compliment.

We read in the book of Proverbs: "Anxiety in the heart of man causes depression, / But a good word makes it glad" (12:25). And "Pleasant words are like a honeycomb, / Sweetness to the soul and health to the bones" (16:24). Don't you love it when someone says something to encourage you? That's how much others enjoy being encouraged by you.

Truth in Love: Ephesians 4:15 teaches that we are to be "speaking the truth in love," but that's hard to do. We have a great deal of trouble keeping our balance. We want to either speak the truth without love, or we want to speak love without truth.

Even if you know something is true, you might not be the best one to share it if you cannot do it in love.

It is extremely difficult for me to say anything to anyone if it might hurt him or embarrass him. Yet if there is something in a friend's life hurting him that could be corrected, the loving thing for me to do is to tell him.

For example, if you had the habit of smacking your lips when you eat, and that single quality was keeping you from getting a promotion, wouldn't you want to know? That would be an easy thing to correct, and it would be a big favor if someone brought it to your attention.

Again, Proverbs says, "Open rebuke is better / Than love carefully concealed. / Faithful are the wounds of a friend, / But the kisses of an enemy are deceitful" (27:5-6).

So we see that it is the duty of a loving friend to tell someone the truth, even if it hurts. Therefore, if someone comes to you with truth that is hard to hear, the thing to do is hear it anyway. Proverbs 15:31 says, "The ear that hears the rebukes of life / Will abide among the wise."

The key is that what is said must be truth, and it must be said in love. Even if you know something is true, you might not be the best one to share it if you cannot do it in love. Galatians 6:1 says that "if a man is overtaken in any trespass, you who are spiritual restore such a one in a spirit of gentleness, considering yourself lest you also be tempted."

From this passage we learn that if the truth is a matter of a person's sin, the individual who takes the truth to the sinner must be spiritually mature. And in any event the truth must be told gently, realizing we ourselves might later be on the receiving end of such a message.

Good Reports: One of the most uplifting things we can hear is when someone tells us something good someone said about us. Perhaps you are a parent, and your child's teacher has told you what a good student he or she is in math. Don't keep that information to yourself; share it with your child. Suppose you hear someone say a person taught a really good Sunday school class. Go tell the person. A good report is a powerful way to say words that help.

Cheerfulness: Would you rather be around a cheerful person or a cheerless person? Unless you are highly unusual, you would rather be around a cheerful person. Why? Well, because they are so . . . cheerful.

Negative people drag us down. Positive people lift us up. Cheerful people fill us with encouragement, hope, pleasure, and good will.

Therefore, if you want to speak words that help, be cheerful. No one enjoys being around a complainer, or a grouser, or a nitpicker.

Become a person whose words help and heal.

Think about your speech. Do you lie (how about exaggerate)? Do you get angry? Do you gossip? Do you swear or use vulgar language? Are you true to your word? If you say something, can others count on its being true?

On the other hand, do you encourage others? Do you tell the truth in love? Do you give good reports to others, and are you cheerful?

The Lord wants to clean your heart of hurtful speech. It is for your own good as well as the Lord's reputation that your heart be cleaned up and your language reflect the cleansing.

Study your speech. Be honest with yourself. Ask the Holy Spirit to pinpoint your weaknesses and to strengthen you to overcome them. Then commit yourself to being a person whose words help, not hurt.

Life-Check

1. How would you characterize your speech? Do you see your-self as someone who is known for helpful speech or hurtful speech?

2. If you are married, how do you think your spouse would characterize your speech? If you aren't married, how would your parents or good friends characterize your speech? Are you a person who is known for hurtful speech or helpful speech?

3. Of the hurtful speech characteristics in this chapter, which is your greatest weakness? How do you think you can begin to overcome that weakness?

4. Of the helpful speech characteristics in this chapter, which is your greatest strength? How do you think you can capital-ize on it?

5. When you say something, are you consistently true to your word? If you are or are not, how do you think that impacts you?

For Further Reflection

Scripture

Proverbs 12:22
Proverbs 16:24
Luke 6:45
Ephesians 4:15
Ephesians 4:29
Ephesians 5:4

James 1:19-20
James 3:2-6
1 Timothy 5:13
Proverbs 27:5-6
Proverbs 15:31
Proverbs 12:25

Books

Tongue in Check, Joseph Stowell
That's Not What I Meant, Tim Stafford

10

Seeking God Instead of the Top of the Ladder

Success is being faithful to what God asks
of us and leaving the results to Him.

This Book of the Law shall not depart from your
mouth, but you shall meditate in it day and
night, that you may observe to do according
to all that is written in it. For then you will
make your way prosperous, and then you
will have good success.
Joshua 1:8

I have always been fascinated by dogsled racing. I'm not sure why. I think it has something to do with the stark man-against-the-enemy, do-or-die, winner-take-all circumstances and the almost mystical bond that develops between a musher (dogsled racer) and his dogs. So it was with unusual interest that I read about author Gary Paulsen, a Minnesotan who, having never run a dogsled race and having put in only 150 training miles with his dog team in the familiar Minnesota woods, ran the 1,200-mile Iditarod dogsled race from Anchorage to Nome, Alaska, in the dead of winter.

In a fit of naiveté bordering on insanity brought on after some amateur sledding one day, Paulsen decided to enter the race on a course that, he would later learn, would nearly kill him several times. He immediately started his team on endurance training, and the first day turned out to be a microcosm of his entire sledding career. Had he known that, I feel sure he would have quit right then. When all the dogs were hitched to the sled, he went to the rig, stood by it, waved to his wife who was watching by the door of the house, and jerked the rope holding the sled to a tree. The dogs bolted.

> I don't think the rig hit the ground more than twice all the way across the yard. *My* [*word*], I thought, *they've learned how to fly*. With me hanging out the back like a tattered flag, we came to the end of the driveway, where we would have to turn onto the road.

> The dogs made the turn fine. The rig started to turn as well, but I had forgotten to lean into the corner, and it rolled over. We set off along the road with the rig upside down, and me dragging in the gravel on my face.

> It took me four miles to get the rig up on its wheels, by which time the handlebar was broken off and I had nothing to hang on to but the steering ropes. I was also nearly completely denuded, my clothes having been torn into shreds during the dragging.

We did the thirty mile [training run] in just under two and a half hours, and never once was I in anything like even partial control of the situation.

In subsequent outings I left the yard on my face, my rear, my back, my belly. One day I left the yard with wooden matches in my pocket that ignited while I was being dragged as I passed the door of the house. It gave me the semblance of a meteorite, screaming something about my pants being on fire—while Ruth laughed so hard she couldn't stand up.[1]

Paulsen never gave up, though. He ran the two-week-long Iditarod race and finished. An astonishing feat. The training runs were a stroll in the park by comparison. When he crossed the finish line, a reporter asked him if he had anything to say. He said, "I'm coming back next year and winning." He did come back the next year. But he didn't win. He has since wisely retired and lives as a writer in New Mexico.

Americans are preoccupied with success, which is often interpreted as being number one.

He never won the race he said he would win. Was he a failure because he didn't win? Or was he a success simply because he did his best? What is success? Can you fail at the task and still succeed? And for the Christian, how does God view success? Can we fail at the task and still succeed in God's eyes? Is it enough just to finish the course, or must we win?

Americans are preoccupied with success, which is often interpreted as being number one. Football players shove their faces into the lenses of sideline cameras, hold up their index finger, and shout "We're number one!" Is that success?

Each year, *Fortune* magazine publishes the Fortune 400, a list of the 400 richest individuals in the United States. Is that success? My *alma mater* sends out a regular mailing listing the achievements of its graduates, and there are many stories of her children having done well. Is that success?

Just what is success? Is it possible for everyone to succeed? How can we know when we have succeeded?

<hr />

Does success satisfy?
Success doesn't satisfy because after we have gotten what we want, we want something more.

The world defines success broadly: getting what you want. If you do, you are a success. If you don't, you aren't. The problem with the world's success is that the *eyes of man are never satisfied* (Prov. 27:20). The world's success is a carrot on a stick. When you take a step toward it, it moves. So you have to decide whether or not you are going to be a donkey.

I remember when I first went to college not far from my hometown, my vision for my life after I graduated was to move back to my hometown, live in some newly built apartments, and teach high school English. When I got a few years into college, I wanted to finish graduate school and then move back to teach in the college and live in some apartments close to campus. When I graduated and went to graduate school, I wanted to teach in a Bible college or seminary.

Then my life changed course, and I went into the pastorate of a brand-new church, totally satisfied if it never grew. I just wanted to be faithful to the people God brought to us. But before long I became frustrated with the lack of growth, and greener pastures appealed to me. Later I pastored a large church that experienced meteoric growth. But there was a church not far away growing even faster. I am a slow learner, but it finally dawned even on me that the finish line kept moving. The sad thing was I was the one who moved it.

When I first started writing, I was happy just to get a publisher. Then after I had written a few books I was no longer happy just getting a book published. I wanted it to sell well (for the Lord's glory, of course). Then I started comparing my books with other writers and felt mine were deficient. I wanted to write prophetic fire as well as Charles Colson and drop pearls of spiritual wisdom as well as Charles Swindoll. I even thought of changing my name to Charles. But I also wanted to be able to pen profound theology like James Packer and sow family life insight like James Dobson. Maybe if I changed my name to Charles James? Then Max Lucado's books started doing well, and I didn't know what to do!

The Holy Spirit eventually let it dawn on me that Charles Colson cannot write like James Dobson and James Packer cannot write like Chuck Swindoll, and I will never write like any of them. I'm crazy if I want to be able to span the breadth of all of them. We each have a gift, a calling, a niche to fill. We are only to be faithful at what God wants us to do. If we lose our grip on that, we can end up on a treadmill leading to nowhere.

Needing to be a success is a deadly trap, and Satan will use it to destroy us if we let him. We must let go of the need to succeed. I don't think it is necessarily wrong to desire success if it is for right reasons, and I don't think it is wrong to work hard to achieve it. But when we *need* it, we're in trouble.

Is success necessary?
Success isn't necessary because God loves us for who we are, not what we accomplish.

One of the greatest things to learn in life is that, by God's definition, success isn't necessary. Each of us has inherent and infinite worth because, and only because, we are created in the image of God. We are already a success in God's eyes. We are a success not because of what we accomplish but because of who we are. His creation. His child. His adopted heir. One for whom He died. God created us so that He could have a relationship with us, so He could be kind to us forever, so He could prove to the world through us that He is who He says He is . . . omnipotent, omniscient, omnipresent, loving, just, kind, holy, and good. He wants to prove to the universe *through us* that He is all these things.

If we insist on pursuing success as a measure of our worth, then two unpleasant things may happen. First, circumstances may thwart us. We cannot control people, possessions, and circumstances well enough to guarantee success. Also, if we don't get what we want, we will be unsatisfied because we didn't get it. If we *do* get what we want, we will realize it does not satisfy. Someone said we climb the ladder of success only to find it was leaning against the wrong wall.

God doesn't reward us on the basis of our results. He rewards us on the basis of our faithfulness to Him.

The second unpleasant thing that may happen to us is that God may pry our stubby little fingers, one at a time, off the thing we think will satisfy. He is the only thing (One) who can satisfy us completely and unendingly. And He loves us too much to allow us to go through life blindly trying to find satisfaction in anything besides Himself. He may induce failure so we will learn to transfer our affections to Him (Hebrews 12:5-11).

How can we achieve true success?
We can achieve true success by being faithful to God and leaving the results to Him.

In Joshua 1:8, God tells us what it takes to succeed:

> This Book of the Law shall not depart from your mouth, but you shall meditate in it day and night, that you may observe to do according to all that is written in it. For then you will make your way prosperous, and then you will have good success.

We can see it a little more clearly if we think through the passage backwards. For us to make our way prosperous and successful, we must do according to all that is written in the Book of the Law. In order to do all that is written in it, we must study and meditate on it continuously. *So, success comes when we are faithfully obedient to God's Word.* All we must do is discern as well as we can what God wants us to do and do it. That is success.

All the results belong to God. The apostle Paul wrote in 1

Corinthians 3:6, "I planted, Apollos watered, but God gave the increase." This only reinforced the words of Jesus recorded by John, "without Me you can do nothing" (John 15:5). We can bear no fruit without the Lord. Why? Because bearing fruit is beyond our ability. Only God can bring forth fruit. But He will use us to produce His fruit if we are faithful to Him.

━━━━━━━━◆━━━━━━━━

God only asks us to be faithful.

The single most discouraging person in the world to me used to be Billy Graham. Don't get me wrong. I admire the man more than I can say. It's just that I couldn't measure up to him, and I wanted to. Shortly after I became a Christian some mentors got me hooked on Billy. I watched him every time he was on television and even went to a crusade. I nearly idolized him. If I could, I wanted to be another Billy Graham.

But I couldn't. I couldn't preach like he could. I couldn't hold a crowd like he could. I never got results like he did. I was so frustrated. I would preach the best sermon that was in me, but no one ever came forward or became a Christian. I would say, "Lord, it isn't fair. Billy Graham is going to get a fabulous mansion in heaven for his reward, and I am going to live in a tar-paper shack. I can't help it if I'm not as gifted as Billy Graham. I can't help it if the Holy Spirit chooses to work through him and not through me. I can't help it if my fruit isn't as great as his is. It isn't fair." It used to drive me nuts.

I didn't realize one fundamental truth. God doesn't reward us on the basis of our results. He rewards us on the basis of our faithfulness to Him. He is the one who determines results.

God may ask someone to work in an inner-city mission where circumstances are discouraging and recognition from others is nonexistent. If He does, that person can be 100 percent faithful to that call, or 50 percent faithful to that call, or 0 percent faithful to that call. And God will reward him according to his faithfulness.

Then, God may call a man like Billy Graham to a ministry that is very public, has phenomenal response, and leads to worldwide recognition. And Billy can be 100 percent faithful to that call, or 50 percent faithful, or 0 percent faithful. And God will reward him according to his faithfulness. We all have an equal ability to be faithful. Therefore, God can reward everyone equally, potentially.

God wants to bring us to the place where we realize that success doesn't satisfy and defeat doesn't destroy. The only thing that matters is whether we get up in the morning and say, "Lord, what do you want me to do today?" and whether we can lie down at night and say "I did it." That is true success.

To the person who lives that way, God adds love, joy, and peace—the fruits of the Spirit. There is great freedom in not needing to succeed. Not only are we free from the anguish of comparison and feelings of failure, but we can also then be trusted. When we don't need to succeed God can, if He chooses, trust us with results that look to the world like success but are only a sovereign decision by God to use us and have nothing whatsoever to do with our worth or our eternal reward. He can put something in our hands and trust we will not clutch it to our breast and call it ours.

Life-Check

1. What is your greatest area of temptation for the world's success? In what ways do you get tricked into "walking after the carrot" of success?

2. Do you feel comfortable believing that God loves you simply because of who you are and not because of what you can accomplish? Think of someone you love. Do you love him or her because of what he or she has accomplished or because of who he or she is? Why is it difficult for Christians to relax in the confidence that God loves us unconditionally?

3. If we cannot produce spiritual results, should we be concerned? Why or why not?

For Further Reflection

Scripture

Joshua 1:8
1 Corinthians 3:6
John 15:5
Proverbs 27:20
Hebrews 12:5-11

Books

Grace Awakening, Chuck Swindoll
30 Days to Understanding How To Live as a Christian, Max Anders

11

The Law of Forgiveness:
Clean Up Your Act

You must be willing to forgive and be forgiven
or your wounds will never heal and your
conscience will never be clear.

Be kind to one another, tenderhearted,
forgiving one another, even as God in
Christ forgave you.
Ephesians 4:32

*F*orgiveness is one of the most powerful forces in the world. Without it we are wounded, crippled, and enslaved. With it we can be healed, strengthened, and set free. A dramatic example of this was seen in the life of Ronald Woomer, known as Rusty, who was condemned to the electric chair in South Carolina for murder.

On April 27, 1990, Rusty sat on the edge of his narrow prison-cell bunk on South Carolina's death row, his head and right leg shaved slick and moistened with conducting gel to help the 2,000 volts of electricity enter his body and kill him for having committed brutal, senseless crimes.

Five years earlier, Rusty had sat comatose on the floor of his cell in such despair that when cockroaches crawled over his lap and shoulders, he didn't even bother to flick them off.

Prison Fellowship volunteer Bob McAlister, deputy chief of staff for the governor of South Carolina, sat down on the floor outside Rusty's cell and tried to talk to him. He did not respond. He sat motionless, looking but not seeing, filthy, degraded, and utterly without hope. He had died already. Only his heart had not stopped beating.

McAlister wrote:

> Frustrated and scared, I prayed aloud that God would cut through the evil in that cell and pierce the heart of its inhabitant.
>
> "Rusty, just say the word *Jesus*," I pleaded.
>
> With much effort, he pursed his lips together and whispered, "Jesus."
>
> "Just look at you," I gently chided. "Your cell's filthy and so are you. The roaches have taken over and you're spiritually a dead man, son. Jesus can give you something better."
>
> I asked Rusty if he wanted to accept Jesus as Lord and Savior. Through tears, he nodded, then prayed. "Jesus, I've hurt a lot of

people. Ain't no way that I deserve You to hear me. But I'm tired and I'm sick and I'm lonely. My mama's died and she's in heaven with You, and I never got to tell her bye. Please forgive me, Jesus, for everything I've done. I don't know much about You, but I'm willin' to learn, and I thank You for listenin' to me."

Forgiveness is one of the most powerful forces in the world.

I went back to see him the next Monday. I walked up to his cell; it was spotless. Gone were the dirt and roaches and porno magazines. The walls were scrubbed, the bed was made, and the scent of disinfectant hung in the air.

"Bob, how do you like it?" exclaimed a smiling, energized Rusty. "I spent all weekend cleaning out my cell 'cause I figured that's what Jesus wanted me to do."

"Rusty," I blurted, "it took you all weekend to clean out your cell, but it took Jesus an instant to clean out your life."

Rusty and I became brothers in Christ. He loved to sit and listen as I read the Bible. During these quiet times of Bible reading, talking, and praying over four-and-a-half years, I hope I taught Rusty something about living. He taught me how to die.

As his appeals were turned down and his execution became a certainty, Rusty developed a simple vision of the hereafter: "When I get to heaven, Jesus and my mama are gonna be waitin' for me," he would say in his thick West Virginia drawl. "And my mama and me are gonna go fishin'."

[Hours before his execution], Rusty prayed, "Our precious Lord, I'm not crying 'cause I feel bad, but 'cause I'm happy. I'm gonna be with You, and You've done everything for me far beyond what I ever deserve. I ask You to watch over my family and take the hurt and sadness from their hearts. I pray that all of this pain and sufferin' will be gone and I just praise You with all of my heart."

The Holy Spirit was doing his final work in Rusty's life—and further work in mine. As we sat there the peace of God washed over us both—a peace that I cannot begin to describe. In that darkened, quiet cell after a frenetic day of emotional upheaval, God chose to move in our hearts, replacing their burdens and fears with the majestic assurance that Rusty would break away from the body of sin and suffering and be whisked away to heaven.

Rusty's body died at 1:05 A.M. that day, but I am convinced that he and his mama are fishin' in heavenly streams.[1]

Oh, my. What a story. What a dramatic example of the power of forgiveness. Before Rusty repented and accepted God's forgiveness, he had degenerated to an animal level, like a swine that doesn't bother to swat away the flies. But when he repented, was born again, and accepted the forgiveness Jesus offered him, he took off like a rocket on a steady, upward course of becoming like Christ.

It is difficult to overstate the power of forgiveness. Unless we are willing to forgive, our wounds will never heal. Unless we are willing to repent and be forgiven, our conscience will never be clear. In these simple facts lies one of the most profound truths of human existence and one of the most commonly missed. An unwillingness to forgive, or an unwillingness or inability to accept forgiveness, has robbed the joy from as many lives as almost any other spiritual problem.

❖

Why must we repent and seek forgiveness when we sin?

Because God commands it, and because without forgiveness we lose our moral authority and remain in bondage to the sin.

God commands forgiveness because it's what we need. In Matthew we read, "Therefore if you bring your gift to the altar, and there remember that your brother has something against you, leave your gift there before the altar, and go your way. First be reconciled to your brother, and then come and offer your gift" (Matt. 5:23-24).

It couldn't be much clearer. But repenting of sin is hard. Confessing it is harder. Asking for forgiveness is even harder.

As a result, we rarely do it. And our failure gets us into big trouble.

Many years ago when I was in seminary, there were two freight trains on the track of my life, rushing straight for a head-on collision. The first train was my study of the Hebrew language, the original language of the Old Testament. Hebrew is a difficult language to master. Rule number one in studying Hebrew? Never get behind! Period. If you do, you're done for. It takes all the time you have to keep up, and you cannot keep up and catch up at the same time.

I was getting behind. Why? The other freight train on my track, money. In addition to having trouble with Hebrew, I was also having trouble with money. In fact, I had too much Hebrew and not enough money! So when I had the chance to work overtime near the end of a semester, I took it. I began working forty to forty-five hours a week just before final exams at the end of my second year. I knew it was a risk, but I didn't know what else to do.

> *Unless we are willing to forgive,*
> *our wounds will never heal.*

I was able to keep up with all my classes except Hebrew. I got behind and couldn't catch up.

The course rule was this: No matter what your daily grades and other exam scores were, you had to pass the final exam or you could not pass the course. And you had to pass the course to graduate from seminary. It was offered only once a year, so if I failed this course, I would have to stay in seminary another year just to make up one Hebrew course. That was unthinkable. I couldn't afford it financially or emotionally. To say the least, a lot was riding on this final exam, and I doubted if I could pass it.

When the fateful day came, the instructors herded all the sections of second-year Hebrew into one small room to take the test at the same time. The room was too small. The chairs were the old wooden kind with a right-armed desk top. To get us all in, they had to push the chairs so close together that they touched.

Did you know that if you cup your hand on your forehead just above your eyes, you can look through the cracks in your fingers and see perfectly clearly, though no one can see where you're looking? You appear to be concentrating diligently on the paper on your desk, but you can see the papers on both sides of you if you switch hands. The guy on my left was a whiz kid. He was translating the Hebrew with little more effort than it would take me to read Dr. Seuss. I wrote what he wrote, and then I double-checked his accuracy with the guy on my right, who was no slouch either. I even slipped in a few deliberate mistakes of my own, so my paper wouldn't be exactly like anyone else's. I wasn't greedy. I didn't need an A. All I needed was a C.

I thought I was saved. I would pass the course and graduate from seminary.

Surprisingly, my cheating brought only minor twinges of conscience, because I felt my personal circumstances had backed me into an impossible corner. I figured it was easier to get forgiveness than permission. So I cheated, told the Lord I was sorry, and went on with my life.

Several months later I had the profound misfortune of attending a seminar in which the leader talked about cleansing your conscience and how a clear conscience is the basis of all moral authority. I had been to this seminar several times before and knew that he always talked about this, but I had forgotten. If I had remembered, I never would have attended.

When the teacher got to the "cleansed conscience" part, I began to get uncomfortable. My discomfort resembled the feeling you have when you remember you are going to the dentist. I began to fidget. My heart began to race. Little beads of sweat broke out on my forehead. The Holy Spirit was putting me in a great spiritual vice and cranking down the pressure: "If you want to be like Jesus, you cannot cheat your way out of problems! Pastors' lives are not built on dishonesty! You have sinned against God, violated the standards of the school, and damaged your own moral authority!"

I was in big trouble, and I knew it. Again, I was faced with two impossible choices. Either I could spit in the face of God and reject His work in my heart, or I could go back to my Hebrew professor and confess to him that I had cheated. I felt a little of what David wrote about in Psalm 32 after one of his great sins:

> When I kept silent, my bones grew old
> Through my groaning all the day long.
> For day and night Your hand was heavy upon me;
> My vitality was turned into the drought of summer. (vv. 3-4)

After an eternity of wrestling with God, pleading with Him to let me off the hook, promising that I would never do it again, and having God stonewall me, I finally broke. I confessed my sin on a deep level, acknowledged my lack of trust in Him, asked for forgiveness, and agreed with God to make it right.

I made an appointment with my Hebrew professor to tell him what I had done. I didn't know what would happen. At the least, I would fail the class, have to stay in school another year to make it up, and graduate a year late. At worst, I could be kicked out of seminary. Maybe my transgression would go on my transcript, and whenever I tried to get a job in a church, a letter from the seminary would say, "Overall, he was a decent student, but the little stinker will cheat if you let him." Maybe they would stamp that sentence on my forehead.

If we don't ask for forgiveness when we wrong someone, we lose our moral authority.

When I finished my story, the professor (may his tribe increase!) said, "Well, Max, I think you have learned a lesson more important than Hebrew. I'll make a deal with you. Since there were extenuating circumstances, I will give you an incomplete for this course, and if you take the next required Hebrew course and pass it, I will give you a 'C' for this course. How is that?"

My first impulse was to clutch his ankles and weep quietly on his shoe tops. Instead, I merely said, "That would be fine. Thank you." And I walked out of his office.

I felt deeply cleansed. Pure. Holy. I wanted to laugh and cry at the same time. I wanted to run and jump and dance. The burden was lifted. The chains were broken. I was free!

I was so deeply grateful to God, not because the worst hadn't happened. I was prepared for that. I was filled with joy because I felt forgiven. God would not let me sweep my sin under the rug where it would rot like old cheese. He loved me enough to make me go through the pain of correcting it Jesus' way. Now, no one could ever say to me, "You cheated, and you never made it right."

If we don't ask for forgiveness when we wrong someone, we lose our moral authority; the debris of sin begins to accumulate in our hearts, choking our conscience, and we lose our reputation as a person of integrity. Others know when we sin against them, and if we don't make it right, it hurts our reputation as well as God's.

Forgiveness is a two-edged sword. I have only put my thumb to one edge so far—namely, that we must repent and seek forgiveness when we sin. We look now at the second edge.

<hr />

Why must we be willing to forgive others when they sin against us?
If we do not forgive others when they sin against us, our emotional wounds will never heal.

In Matthew 18:21-22, Peter asked Jesus how many times he ought to forgive the brother who sins against him. "Up to seven times?" he asked, probably thinking he had really gone the extra mile. Jesus responded, "I do not say to you, up to seven times, but up to seventy times seven."

In the Lord's prayer, when Jesus taught His disciples to pray, He included "And forgive us our debts, / As we forgive our debtors" (Matt. 6:12).

The hurt others inflict on us and the resentment it generates is one of the hardest things in the Christian life to get over. You may want revenge—an eye for an eye, or worse. You may want to vindicate yourself. You may want to let the world see that it was the other person and not you who was wrong. There are countless ways we can be hurt and an equal number of forms our bitterness and resentment can take.

Our bitterness and resentment bubbles, boils, and stews in our hearts until the unholy mess fills our lives with a stench. Then we eat the mess over the days, weeks, months, or years. The chief drawback is that what we are consuming is ourselves. The carcass after the meal is us. Often the other person(s) knows nothing about our hurt, or if they do, have effortlessly ignored it. We are the ones who suffer. The pain dominates our lives. It disrupts other relationships (Heb. 12:14-15). It costs us sleep, peace, and normal living.

There is only one way to stop the self-inflicted carnage. We must forgive. That's not to say that we shouldn't take steps to correct a wrong, but whatever action we take, we must first forgive. It is, as I said, one of the hardest things in the Christian life to do, but one of the most necessary.

Often, forgiveness is an act of the will that is followed by a process. Like Frankenstein's monster, resentment comes to life again. That doesn't mean we didn't forgive in the first place. It just means that whenever we are tempted to take up the offense again, we must forgive again—or remind ourselves that we have already forgiven and are not going to take up the offense again.

Forgiveness is essential to freedom.

This principle is one of the most important in the Christian life. Without it we are a slave to our past. With it we are free in Christ.

Forgiveness is so hard, yet so necessary. It is necessary for us to seek forgiveness from those we have wronged, or we will never have a clear conscience. It is necessary for us to forgive those who hurt us, or our wounds and relationships will never heal.

Forgiveness is an act of the will, and we can forgive regardless of the inclination of our heart. Does someone come to mind who has hurt you? Have you forgiven him or her? If not, do so now. Does someone come to mind whom you have wronged? Pray and ask the Lord what you should do to correct it.

Life-Check

1. Are you struggling with hurt and/or resentment over something someone did to you? Have you forgiven him or her or them? If not, is there any reason you could not forgive them now?

2. Have you forgiven someone who's hurt you but find the feelings of anger and resentment returning? (Heb. 12:15) Did you realize that forgiveness can be a process after the initial act? Is there any reason why, if you need to, you could not forgive again, or perhaps remind yourself that you have already forgiven, so that you are not manipulated by your emotions?

3. Is there anyone you need to ask for forgiveness? Is there any reason why you could not determine to ask that person to forgive you as soon as practical? Is there any restitution you need to offer?

4. Do you feel the lack of moral authority associated with a conscience that isn't clear? Would you like to experience the freedom and joy of a clear conscience? Are you willing to make the sacrifice?

For Further Reflection

Scripture

Matthew 6:9-13
Matthew 18:15-35
2 Corinthians 2:3-11
Ephesians 4:29-32
Hebrews 12:15
Matthew 5:23-24
Psalm 32:3-4

Books

The Freedom of Forgiveness, David Augsburger

12

The Law of Relationships:
Find a Hand to Hold

It is people, not things,
that make life worthwhile.

Greater love has no one than this,
than to lay down one's life for his friends.
John 15:13

*E*arly in his administration, President Ronald Reagan came out of the Hilton hotel where he had spoken and was walking a short distance to his car when he heard a noise—*pop, pop, pop*—like firecrackers going off. His Secret Service bodyguard shoved him into the nearby presidential limousine and jumped in on top of him. Reagan felt a crushing pain in his ribs and thought that his bodyguard had broken a rib when he jumped on top of him. Only later did he learn that the pain was from a gunshot wound.

When you strip everything away, life really comes down to this: knowing we are not alone, knowing somebody cares, knowing we are loved.

He began coughing up blood, and they rushed him to George Washington Hospital. He was walking to the emergency room when he got lightheaded and weak in the knees. He was also having great difficulty breathing. The next thing he knew he was lying face up on a gurney, being wheeled into the hospital. Later as he was going into the operating room, he looked at the surgical team and quipped, "I sure hope you're all Republicans."

Before he went into the operating room, however, while he was still in the emergency room, Reagan's difficulty with breathing increased. His lungs were working, but no matter how many times he took a breath, he couldn't get enough air, even though the E.R. staff had an oxygen tube down his throat. He began to panic and finally blacked out.

When President Reagan regained consciousness some time later he felt someone, evidently one of the nurses, holding his hand. He later wrote, "It is difficult for me to describe how deeply touched I was by that gesture. It was very reassuring just to feel the warmth of a human hand." He was still not fully conscious and could not see who was holding his hand, giving him such a surge of encouragement. "Who's holding my hand?" he asked. There was no answer. "Who's holding my hand?" he asked again. Again, no answer. "Does Nancy know about us?"[1]

When you strip everything away, life really comes down to this: knowing we are not alone, knowing somebody cares, knowing we are loved.

Why are relationships so important?
God created in us a need for meaningful relationships, and unless we have them, life becomes very unsatisfying.

Harold Kushner, in his book *When All You Ever Wanted Isn't Enough*, wrote:

> I was sitting on a beach one summer day, watching two children, a boy and a girl, playing in the sand. They were hard at work, building an elaborate sand castle by the water's edge, with gates and towers and moats and internal passages. Just when they had nearly finished their project, a big wave came along and knocked it down, reducing it to a heap of wet sand. I expected the children to burst into tears, devastated by what had happened to all their hard work. But they surprised me. Instead, they ran up the shore away from the water, laughing and holding hands, and sat down to build another castle. I realized that they had taught me an important lesson. All the things in our lives, all the complicated structures we spend so much time and energy creating are built on sand. Only our relationships to other people endure. Sooner or later, the wave will come along and knock down what we have worked so hard to build up. When that happens, only the person who has somebody's hand to hold will be able to laugh.[2]

God has created us to live in harmony and unity with other humans, and unless we have meaningful relationships, life becomes hard for us.

Billy Graham has often said that the number-one most popular sermon he preaches is on loneliness. In our look-out-for-number-one society, we have gotten what we looked out for: ourselves. And we find that *we* are not enough to satisfy ourselves. We feel alienated, isolated, lonely.

We have become a highly mobile society, moving at the drop of a hat for more money or better weather or prettier scenery. But because we're so transient, we never get rooted; we never get a sense of belonging. We never rid ourselves of the loneliness. Why? Because people are what make life worth living.

So, we had better begin looking out for what we really want: others. Life is only meaningful if we live it *with* and *for* others.

What does it take to have friends?
To have a friend, you must be a friend.

Many of my friends are the opposite of me. I am highly people-oriented, talkative, and enjoy high-energy, high-profile activities. Many of my friends are quiet, reserved, and introspective. Not that I don't have friends who are like me. I do. The point is, friendships can occur in unlikely as well as likely contexts. All it takes is two people with at least one common interest significant enough to hold them together.

I take great delight in talking with people who are experts in areas I know nothing about. They enjoy talking about their area of expertise, and I enjoy hearing about it. Being genuinely interested in other people is the surest way I know to develop friends.

> **Life is only meaningful if we live it with and for others.**

Perhaps the single greatest deterrent to making friends is television. It becomes too easy to fall under the spell of the magic box that entertains us twenty-four hours a day. In years gone by, when the day ended and dinner was finished, people sat on the front porch or went for walks or visits. Now we collapse into our most comfortable chair and flip on the tube. It numbs our brain until we finally rise to go to bed. It does nothing to foster friendships. In fact, it robs us of the time and energy to do things that would enlarge our circle of friends. People who have a great many friends are not tied to the tube.

Where can we find friends?
Our family, church, workplace, neighborhood, and community are rich potential sources of friendships.

Sometimes family is a good source of friendship. I have good friends within my family, and I know others who do also. If we have friends in our family, we should think carefully before moving away.

My brother turned his back on a promising career as an electronics engineer because he would rather live close to his extended family, despite the fact that there were no employment opportunities for electronic engineers in the area. I applaud his decision though I know that not everyone has the option to do what he did.

Sometimes, for various reasons, family doesn't afford the best opportunity to have friends. In that case people in our church can fill the role we might wish the family could play. In the churches I have pastored it isn't uncommon to hear people say, "This church is my family." One should be cautious about giving that up.

Before I began pastoring, my wife and I moved a couple of times in search of a church that we could mesh with. It made for a lonely time. Short of the Lord's clear leading, I would never move again unless I thought there was a reasonable chance to become integrated into a good church.

Other times we find good friends at work or across the street in our neighborhood or at Little League practice. The potential sources for friendships are many, and we can have friends if we can make friends and do not move away from them unnecessarily.

C.S. Lewis wrote:

> Friendship is the greatest of worldly goods. Certainly to me it is the chief happiness of life. If I had to give a piece of advice to a young [person] about a place to live, I think I should say, "Sacrifice almost everything to live where you can be near your friends."[3]

Sometimes God doesn't give us the option of staying where our friends are. Circumstances require us to move away. We may be in the military. Or we may be a pastor or missionary, and the will of God mandates our move to a new location. An inability to find employment in one location could force a move.

But in general, I think people move too often for insufficient reasons and don't give the issue of relationships adequate weight in evaluating the move. Then, when they get where they are going, they often feel alienated, alone, and detached, especially if they don't make new friends easily. Just as our bodies need food and water, so our souls need other people to nourish and sustain us.

What happens when we have inadequate relationships?
When we are not properly connected with other people, it spawns other problems.

Loneliness, alienation, and rootlessness, which are painful enough in themselves, make us susceptible to other problems. Just as insects and disease always attack the weakest flowers in the garden, so spiritual and emotional problems seem to afflict more readily those already struggling with fundamental problems like loneliness and alienation. Marital infidelity, depression, overspending, moral lapses, and other crises more easily materialize in the weakened condition of one who doesn't have enough true friends.

The Richness of Friendship

If we are secure in whom God created us to be, and secure in who we are in Christ, we bring something valuable to all our relationships. We see people as individuals to whom we can manifest the character and/or proclaim the name of Christ. Out of the reservoir of security from being a child of God, we can help others experience their own significance and security. When this happens, we become a "friendship machine," churning out friendships faster than we're able to sustain them. As a result, we may have several different levels of friendship.

We may have intimate, lifelong friends, with whom we can share the joys and sorrows of life. Sometimes we are fortunate enough to live near these friends, and they are part of our ongoing life. Other times we may live apart from these friends, but whenever we get the opportunity to see them, we pick up the friendship immediately as though no time had passed since we last saw them. There are a limited number of people with whom we can sustain a close, intimate relationship, since close friendships take time. But whether these friends live in the same area we do or not, they bring great richness to our lives.

God intended us to live our lives converting as many enemies into friends as possible.

A level down from intimate, lifelong friends are our good friends. These are people we enjoy, but for whatever reason, we don't have that intimate relationship with them that would make them lifelong friends if we moved away. We can have more of these kinds of friends because the time commitment is not as great as with intimate friends.

Next, we may have casual friends. These are people who cross our paths as a result of our everyday life. They may be coworkers, neighbors, parents of children who are friends with our children, or someone we play league softball with. We enjoy them when we bump into them, and they enrich our lives, but our relationship remains casual. We can have many of these friends because they come our way in the course of our everyday lives.

Finally, we have acquaintances, people we know but don't have close relationships with. The man I buy gasoline from, the manager of the produce section at the grocery store, the fellow who cuts my lawn, and the usher at church are all people whom I know but don't have a relationship with except in the course of performing my duties. I enjoy seeing them, however, and they bring richness to my life.

When we are secure in our identity as a child of God, we are capable of initiating and sustaining many friendships on various levels, and when we do, we find our lives rich indeed.

If we are not inherently secure in our own identity, we tend to be continually striving to achieve or to prove our worth as a human being. When this happens we tend to see everything, including people, as commodities to be used in the pursuit of our own goals. We see them either as resources to further our goals or obstacles to our goals.

This is a lonely existence and one that is contrary to the will of God. We tend to love things and use people. He wants us to use things and love people. Only when we get this right will life take on the richness God intended us to experience through friends.

During the Civil War Lincoln had occasion at an official reception to refer to the Southerners as erring human beings rather than as foes to be exterminated. An elderly lady, a fiery patriot, rebuked him for speaking kindly of his enemies when he ought to be thinking of destroying them. "Why, madam," said Lincoln, "do I not destroy my enemies when I make them my friends?"

God intended us to live our lives converting as many enemies into friends as possible.

Life-Check

1. Do you have enough friends, or are you lonely, alienated,

rootless? If you do not have enough meaningful relation-ships, why do you think that is true?

2. In the past, what significance have you given to friend-ships? What significance do you think you will give the mat-ter in future decisions?

3. Do you have good friendships in your family? Why or why not? What are ways you might improve your relationships within your family? How about your church?

For Further Reflection

Scripture
Proverbs 18:24
Proverbs 27:10
John 15:13-15

Books
The Friendship Factor, Alan Loy Ginnis
How To Win Friends and Influence People, Dale Carnegie

13

The Law of Nurture:
People Grow Best When Watered with Love

Relationships won't grow unless
you nurture them.

Therefore comfort each other
and edify one another.
1 Thessalonians 5:11

*B*eing from the rich farm country of Indiana, I love the soil. When I was growing up, the soil where we lived seemed to my child's eyes to be so rich that when our family desired a garden, all we had to do was plow up the soil and throw the seeds out on the ground! The next morning we would come out, and the garden would be up and growing. Two days later we would be picking tomatoes and pulling carrots. We grew ears of corn so large that our family of eight could all eat off of one ear at the same time. (It's funny how the longer I'm away, the more fertile that Indiana soil becomes.)

After my wife and I got married, we lived in Phoenix, Portland, and then Atlanta. In Phoenix it was too hot and dry to grow a good garden. In Portland it was too cold and wet. When we got to Atlanta, I was determined to have a garden. The soil in Atlanta is red clay and very acidic. So I talked to some people who ought to know about soil preparation. Following their advice, I tilled into the ground a pile of compost half the size of Pike's Peak. Then I tilled in enough lime (to neutralize the acid in the soil) to dust the state of Rhode Island. Finally, I planted the corn, beans, tomatoes, and zucchini and sat back to wait for harvest day.

As the beans came up, the rabbits held a national convention in our backyard and served our bean sprouts for the main course one night. We never again saw any evidence of having planted beans. The raccoons plucked the corn the instant it developed moisture in the kernels. As we began to see what was happening, we stationed our neighbor's beagle outside at night to scare the varmints off. But the beagle was a sound sleeper, so we reaped no benefit from that.

The tomato plants grew gloriously to about two feet high, developed a profusion of brilliant yellow flowers . . . and fell over dead. Cutworms. We got some powder to get rid of the cutworms, and the two remaining plants began to develop actual tomatoes. They grew to about the size of a peach, turned a delightful light pink, split open, and rotted. Still too much acid in the soil. I should have used enough lime to dust the state of Texas. We never ate a tomato from that garden.

The only vegetable we were able to harvest was zucchini—ten of them. I don't *like* zucchini, but I was able to *grow* it.

It doesn't matter if it is vegetables or personal relationships, nothing grows unless it's nurtured.

We spent about 120 dollars on the garden—composting, tilling, adding lime, more tilling, planting seeds and seedlings, watering, etc. That figures out to about twelve dollars a zucchini. I learned that you can buy a zucchini for considerably less at the grocery store. In fact, I learned that if you know someone with a garden, he can grow zucchini, too, and will give you more than you want even if you *like* it. (The other day in a magazine, I read the warning: "Danger! Keep your car doors locked! It's zucchini season!")

I've never planted another garden. Maybe when we retire we can live in Indiana and have a garden. For now, I am spending my gardening time doing other things.

Just as a garden takes careful nurturing to grow and be healthy, so does everything else. It doesn't matter if it is vegetables or personal relationships—nothing grows unless it's nurtured.

To nurture plants, you must have food, water, sunshine, and protection. To nurture relationships, you must have truth, love, affirmation, and time. If you blow it with your garden, you just end up with twelve-dollar zucchinis and a good story to tell. If you blow it with your spouse or your kids, you may end up with a shattered life.

What is the fundamental principle governing life's key relationships?
We must all give deference to one another.

In Ephesians 5:22-6:9, the apostle Paul discusses three sets of relationships: husband/wife, parent/child, and employer/employee. Husbands are instructed to love their wives as Christ loved the church and gave Himself for her. Wives are to respect their husbands. Parents are to bring their children up in the training and admonition of the Lord. Children are to obey their parents. Employers (masters) are to treat their employees (servants) well, knowing that their own master is in heaven. Employees are to obey their employer and serve him or her as they would Christ.

In each of these relationships there are common principles. First, someone is in authority and someone is in submission. Second, the one in authority is to serve the one in submission. Third, the one in submission is to respect the authority of the one in authority.

The primary responsibility for nurturing key relationships lies on the shoulders of the one in authority—the husband, the parents, and the employer. Certainly, it takes two to tango, and an unresponsive wife, child, or employee can thwart the most sincere of efforts. But that doesn't change the principle.

What is the key to happy husband/wife relationships?
The husband is to love his wife as Christ loved the church and gave Himself up for her, while the wife is to respect her husband.

I have seen heartbreaking disintegration of marriages because one or both parties in the marriage failed to nurture the relationship. Sometimes it was out of ignorance, as my disastrous gardening experiment was. Other times it was out of misplaced priorities (jobs, hobbies, money, other people), laziness, or wrong ideas. I have had husbands tell me that their wives left them. It was a bombshell. The husband had no warning. After much conversation, however, in many cases I'd learn that the husband wooed and nurtured his wife until they were married. Then, that job done, he went on to other things. The wife felt abandoned, neglected, unappreciated. After awhile she decided it wasn't worth it. If the husband had spent anywhere near the same time and energy nurturing the relationship *after* marriage as he did *before,* the breakup might never have happened.

That in no way condones a violation of biblical principles in leaving a spouse. It does mean, however, that if you want your marriage to grow, whether you are a husband or a wife, you have to nurture it.

What is the key to successful parent/child relationships?
The parents are to rear their children in the training and admonition of the Lord, while the children are to obey their parents.

Heartbreak among parents over the lives of their children has become epidemic. I can hardly count the times I have seen the children of well-meaning parents go off the deep end and shipwreck or at least seriously damage their lives, and it could have been avoided.

A big problem is absentee fathers. I don't necessarily mean that the mother is a single parent. I also mean that though the father may be living in the same house, he is not significantly involved in the life of the child.

An overemphasis on material success is also a problem. Parents work to support the family financially and often feel that is enough. They don't invest the time, the emotional energy, the mental creativity necessary to build strong relationships with their children. Then they wonder why, when the children become teenagers, they have little to do with the parents and often reject the parents' value system. The reason is that their peer group has begun to exert a greater influence in their lives than the parents, and the parental relationship suffers greatly.

Inadequate or undemonstrated love between parents is another problem. A husband and wife's greatest devotion in life, after the Lord, must be to each other. The greatest gift they can give their children is a home where the love between the husband and wife is secure and obvious. After that the children must be the number one priority.

Imagine a lifeguard sitting in his lifeguard chair getting a glorious tan, when suddenly a swimmer needs help. The lifeguard shouldn't consider that an interruption. The swimmers are his primary responsibility. Similarly, parents need to sit on a high chair in life, looking out over the beach for their children, making sure everything is okay with them. If the children need something, it should not be considered an interruption.

The greatest gift they can give their children is a home where the love between the husband and wife is secure and obvious.

Except for their relationship with the Lord or their spouse, whenever parents place any priority in life higher than their child, the child instinctively understands and looks someplace else for security and significance. This elsewhere is usually their peers. If that happens, the children begin to adopt the value system of their peers, which, if it doesn't include close family ties, will often result in rapid deterioration of the relationships within the family.

A key to healthy parent/child relationships is for the parents to be so positively involved in the lives of their children that the children draw their security and significance as individuals primarily from their relationship with their parents. When that happens, peer influence is significantly reduced, and meaningful family relationships can flourish. This takes time, emotional energy, and mental creativity on the part of the parent(s) devoted to finding out how to have such a relationship with his or her child, as each child is different.

Ephesians 6:4 says not to provoke your children to wrath but to bring them up in the training and admonition of the Lord. Provoking to wrath means to exasperate them. We do this by asking them to do things they can't do, by being inconsistent, by being too protective or not protective enough, and by having too many rules or not enough rules. Rather than exasperating our children, we must bring them up in the training and admonition of the Lord. Training refers to positive instruction and affirmation. Admonition refers to proper correction and discipline when needed.

Even parents who have done a good job of rearing their children will sometimes have a child who rebels against their values. However, they maximize the chances of success if they properly nurture the relationship.

***

What is the key to successful employer/ employee relationships?

The employer is to treat his employees with proper respect, while the employees are to serve their employer.

A revolution is going on in the workplace in America, and while it is certainly not touching every company, it is having a significant impact on employer/employee relationships in many businesses. The revolution is in response to corporate changes the last thirty or forty years. Many employers failed to care about their employees, and as a result, employees failed to care about the product or service they were providing. Productivity and quality both suffered, and American products and productivity, which used to be the envy of the world, became, in many cases, an embarrassment. This not only affects our national pride, it affects our pocketbook. Failing to care about each other and failing to care about our product or service do not pay. Companies cannot thrive long term unless workers care about each other and their tasks. That was one of the major failings of communism. So the revolution is a back-to-basics, love-your-neighbor, care-about-your-work approach to labor and management.

This revolution is welcome because it moves us in the direction of biblical principles. Ephesians 6:5-9 teaches us that we must do our job as though we were working for Christ Himself. Whether we are in labor or management, whether we are an employee or employer, it doesn't matter.

If you are an employer or in management, and you want a better relationship with your workers, putting this principle in action will do two things for you: (1) It will give you happier workers, a more stable work force, a more productive work force, and (2) it will, in the end, be better for your profit/loss statement. But you must work at it. You must find out what the needs of your employees are and do your best to meet those needs, both physical and emotional.

While finances are always important to workers, there is another thing that, in some studies, has proven to be equally important: R-E-S-P-E-C-T! Workers want to know they are valued, appreciated, respected. Good relationships with employees will happen only if those relationships are nurtured by those in authority.

On the other hand, there are things employees can do to nurture relationships also. First, they can respect and honor their employers, working for them as they would Christ. Of course, that means that you don't do illegal or unethical things.

In addition, you must nurture your relationships with coworkers. This is often a significant challenge since some coworkers can be disagreeable. However, Jesus would treat others with respect if He were in our shoes, and therefore, so must we.

Workers want to know they are valued, appreciated, respected.

I remember hearing the story of a tollbooth attendant who was known for her friendliness and efficiency. When asked what the secret was to finding happiness in such a boring job, she replied that shortly after she began working there she realized that if she looked at her job merely as handing out change to people, she would soon go crazy. So she envisioned her job as trying to turn her brief encounters with drivers into opportunities to make their lives a little happier. The money became incidental. She found happiness in her job by serving a higher purpose than her specific function. That is what the Lord wants us to do in the workplace.

Rewarding relationships require careful nurturing.

If we want more than spiritual or emotional "zucchini" to share with people from the garden of our lives, we must nurture our relationships with other people. Henry Wadsworth Longfellow once wrote:

> Kind hearts are the gardens,
> Kind thoughts are the roots;
> Kind words are the flowers.
> Kind deeds are the fruits.
>
> Take care of your garden,
> And keep out the weeds.
> Fill it with sunshine,
> Kind words and kind deeds.

Do you want good relationships? They must be taken care of, nurtured, as must all growing things.

Life-Check

1. How do you think the world would be changed if everyone practiced the principle of mutual deference?

2. If you're married, to what degree do you offer proper deference to your spouse? How has your marriage been affected by your actions? If you're not married but hope to be, how do you think you can live out this principle when you do get married? How did your parents model this principle? How has that affected your own perception and actions?

3. If you have children, how well do you fulfill your obligations to your children? As a child, how well do you fulfill your obligations to your parent(s)?

4. If you work as an employer or manager, how well do you fulfill your biblical obligations to those under your authority? If you are an employee, how well do you fulfill your biblical obligations to those above you?

For Further Reflection
Scripture
Ephesians 5:22-6:9
Colossians 3:18-24
1 Peter 2:18-3:9
1 Thessalonians 5:11
Ephesians 6:4

Books
Straight Talk to Men and Their Wives, James Dobson
What Wives Wish Their Husbands Knew about Women, James Dobson
Dare to Discipline, James Dobson
Love Must Be Tough, James Dobson
Your Work Matters to God, Doug Sherman

14

The Law of Patience:
Instant Gratification Just Doesn't Last

You must be willing to give up a dime today
to gain a dollar tomorrow.

If then you were raised with Christ, seek those
things which are above, where Christ is, sitting
at the right hand of God. Set your mind on
things above, not on things on the earth.
Colossians 3:1-2

*T*he day didn't begin well. Three friends of mine and I decided to explore a pit, which is a vertical cave, way back in the woods where Tennessee, Georgia, and Alabama meet. It was nearly a hundred feet deep and probably forty feet wide, though the opening to it was a deceptively small six-foot-wide hole in the ground. If you didn't know it was there, you could easily walk into it and fall a hundred feet.

For reasons that no longer seem sufficient, we decided to tie a rope around a tree near the opening and do a blind rappel to the bottom. I say blind because you couldn't see a thing going down. Nor was there a cliff to descend, as with most rappelling. Instead, you dropped into the hole as though you were rappelling from a helicopter and free-fell to the bottom.

Our leader, David, went first, followed by another friend. It took a while to rappel that far down, so those of us at the top chatted to pass the time as each person descended. As the second guy was going down, Kelly, my brother-in-law, and I were waiting for him to get to the bottom when I heard a rustle in the leaves on a small rise in the ground just above us. Suddenly, a water moccasin stumbled down the little rise and almost fell into the hole. (I say stumbled because even though I know snakes don't have legs, I don't think he intended to come down the little hill toward us. I think he did the snake equivalent of losing his footing and came sliding clumsily down the little rise toward us.)

This seemed to make him very angry, as though it were our fault. He coiled menacingly, raised his head high, and opened his mouth w-i-d-e. We froze. As I peered bug-eyed into the slimy depths of the water moccasin's venomous gullet, I understood why they are sometimes called cottonmouths. His mouth and throat, as far down as I could see, were white as snow.

My mind was racing now, and I vividly imagined the snake falling into the hole and lodging firmly between our other friend's neck and shirt collar. I shuddered and blinked hard to bring my thoughts back to reality. The snake had not yet fallen into the pit, we didn't want him to fall into the pit, nor did we want him to bite either of us. I fixed a frozen stare on our angry, openmouthed friend.

No matter what the circumstances, there is often a wrong thing to do, which would be quick and easy, and a right thing to do, which is usually time-consuming and hard.

"Go get me a stick," I whispered to Kelly.

Kelly backed away and returned shortly with a switch that wouldn't have threatened a cockroach.

"Get serious!" I hissed. "Get me something that will do some damage!"

The snake and I stared like statues at each other. Kelly was gone a little longer this time but returned with the bottom half of a small tree that had fallen over. That was more like it. I will spare the details, but without digging a hole, I buried that snake in the soft Alabama soil.

I had been a little nervous about this whole cave exploring deal to begin with. Now I was truly spooked. Had I read somewhere that water moccasins always traveled in pairs? I concealed my edginess as Kelly went down next. Finally it was my turn, and I went down uneventfully.

We walked around at the bottom for a while (there really wasn't much to see), took a picture of ourselves to prove we were really there, and began the ascent. To get back up, we had large metal clips strapped to our feet and a harness around our chest that hooked onto the rope, letting the rope slide when the clips were moved up but catching when the clips were moved down. That way, we were able to climb back up the rope to get out.

We had miner's helmets on, but we turned them out to save the batteries going back up. There wasn't anything to see anyway. The great darkness soon swallowed up what little light they gave off. Unlike going down, going up could be done two or three at a time. Though we couldn't see each other, we could feel one another's movements on the rope. Suddenly there was a violent jerking from above me, and Kelly cried out. My blood froze. My heart pounded in my ears. I caught my breath and waited for whatever was going to happen.

I fully expected to see his body drop past me. I hung motionless in the darkness, so afraid I wondered if I could keep my wits about me. I wanted to yell, *"M-o-m-m-y!"* but even in that death-defying situation, I was too embarrassed. For some reason I became firmly convinced that all my clips would give out simultaneously and I would plummet through the darkness to the rocks below. *This is what hell is like,* I thought. *Total darkness. Total aloneness. Total fear.*

As it turned out, Kelly's problem was minor. The clip on one of his shoes had malfunctioned. He made some adjustments, we climbed to the top, and after a quick look around to make sure that water moccasins *didn't* travel in pairs, we went home.

How should we respond to strong emotions?
We should control our emotions, think through the facts, and choose to do what is right.

I learned a good lesson that day: No matter how bad your circumstances are, no matter how great the temptation to ride your emotions like a runaway horse, the best way out is to hold on, to be patient, to grab yourself by the nape of the neck, and make yourself do what you ought to do, in spite of the fact that your emotions might be screaming the opposite message.

More than anything else in the world, I wanted to get out of that situation alive. If I panicked, I diminished my chances. I maximized my chances if I simply grabbed myself by the scruff of the neck and made myself do what I should do. If I had allowed my emotions to make my decisions, either with the snake or the incident on the rope, it could have been life-threatening. As it was, both potential crises were averted.

Real life is sometimes like that pit—filled with darkness and raging terror. Other times it is boring or tedious or frustrating. But no matter what the circumstances, there is often a wrong thing to do, which would be quick and easy, and a right thing to do, which is usually time-consuming and hard. Many of life's decisions fall between these two extremes. Being creatures who prefer instant satisfaction, too often we choose the quick, easy way out and pay dearly later.

As a pastor, I have listened to all too many people's heart-rending stories about messes they were in because they took the quick, easy, and wrong way out of a situation or made the quick, easy, and wrong response to temptation. In America today we have fixated on the quick and easy way.

Daniel Boorstin, former Librarian of Congress and current director of the Smithsonian National Museum of American History, describes current American culture this way:

> When we pick up our newspaper at breakfast, we expect—we even demand—that it bring us momentous events since the night before. We turn on the car radio as we drive to work and expect "news" to have occurred since the morning newspaper went to press. Returning in the evening, we expect our house not only to shelter us, to keep us warm in winter and cool in summer, but to relax us, to dignify us, to encompass us with soft music and interesting hobbies, to be a playground, a theater, and a bar. We expect our two-week vacation to be romantic, exotic, cheap, and effortless. We expect a faraway atmosphere if we go to a nearby place; and we expect everything to be relaxing, sanitary, and Americanized if we go to a faraway place. We expect new heroes every season, a literary masterpiece every month, a dramatic spectacular every week, a rare sensation every night. We expect everybody to feel free to disagree, yet we expect everybody to be loyal, not to rock the boat or take the Fifth Amendment. We expect everybody to believe deeply in his religion, yet not to think less of others for not believing. We expect our nation to be strong and great and vast and varied and prepared for every challenge; yet we expect our "national purpose" to be clear and simple, something that gives direction to the lives of two hundred million people and yet can be bought in a paperback at the corner drugstore for a dollar.

We expect anything and everything. We expect the contradictory and the impossible. We expect compact cars which are spacious; luxurious cars which are economical. We expect to be rich and charitable, powerful and merciful, active and reflective, kind and competitive. We expect to be inspired by mediocre appeals for "excellence," to be made literate by illiterate appeals for literacy. We expect to eat and stay thin, to be constantly on the move, and ever more neighborly, to go to the "church of our choice" and yet feel its guiding power over us, to revere God and to be God.

Instant gratification can bear an exorbitant price tag.

Never have people been more the masters of their environment. Yet never has a people felt more deceived and disappointed.[1]

Is it any wonder that people impatiently run through life led by their emotions like a boxer going through a fight leading with his chin?

What happens when we blindly follow our emotions?
We get into trouble that we otherwise might have avoided.

More times than I care to remember, I have sat in my office as someone told me that he or she was leaving his or her spouse. The person believed it was wrong, thought it was sin, but could not imagine life without another person and was willing to pay whatever price it took down the road for gratification today.

More times than I care to remember, I have sat in my office as a single person told me that he or she was marrying an unbeliever (or someone who claimed to be a believer but who possessed scant evidence to verify it), knowing it was wrong, believing it was sin, yet unable to imagine life without the other person. Many married anyway, believing that it would somehow work out. In most cases, it didn't.

More times than I care to remember, I have sat in my office as people told me about one heartbreaking decision after another in which they were willing to take the quick and easy way out of an emotionally charged situation, blind to the potential consequences down the road, and deaf to the concerns of well-meaning friends.

What our current Christian culture doesn't seem to grasp is that sin is easier up front, but much harder down the road, while righteousness is harder up front, but much easier down the road. For those able and willing to look far enough down the road, good decisions are often easy to make. For those unable or unwilling to look down the road, good decisions don't pay off quickly enough to be convincing, and the only attractive way out is to satisfy their immediate desires.

Instant gratification can bear an exorbitant price tag. Samson is a good example. As a Jew, he wasn't supposed to marry outside his faith. But he asked his father for permission to marry a Gentile woman. His father urged him not to make such a decision, but Samson was committed to his course of action. Later he lived in adultery. In the end it cost him his freedom, his eyesight, his self-respect, and finally, his life.

That is exactly what it will cost us if we aren't careful. Unless we are willing to postpone gratification and patiently seek higher goals, we will be slaves to our whims and appetites and the perilous consequences they bring. If we don't learn this principle, we will be confused and frustrated at God's unwillingness to bless *our* plans and actions, which often backfire in our face.

Whether it is a matter of wisdom or maturity or conscious sin, the principle is the same. Righteousness is always harder up front and easier down the road, and sin is always easier up front and harder down the road.

Exercising patience is hard—but well worth the wait.

Patience doesn't come naturally for me. I remember when I was very young, perhaps four or five years old, and had just eaten a peach. One of my brothers or sisters told me that the seed on the inside was what peach trees grew from. They told me that if

I planted the seed, a peach tree would grow from it and bear more peaches.

Eager to witness this phenomenon, I scurried to the backyard where I planted the peach seed in the sandbox. I slept that night with visions of peach trees dancing in my head. The next morning I went out to the sandbox. There was no peach tree. I was profoundly disappointed. As I stood there, the disappointment grew rapidly to anger. I ripped the peach seed out of the sand and threw it as far as my chubby little fingers could throw it into the field adjoining our backyard. I have been struggling for patience ever since.

I think patience is such a difficult virtue because you don't *do* anything. With the virtue of diligence, you do something. With the virtue of honesty, you do something. But with patience, you don't do anything. You just wait. Most of us don't wait well.

Righteousness is always harder up front and easier down the road, and sin is always easier up front and harder down the road.

Do you have difficulty standing the tension of doing nothing? Do you have difficulty waiting for God's will to become clear to you? Do you have difficulty waiting until some problem is resolved or pain is relieved? Do you have difficulty waiting for a change to happen? Do you ever find yourself saying, "I don't care *what* happens, I just want *something* to happen"?

Patience! Patience!

We need to remind ourselves that God is still in heaven. He is still watching over us. He is still in control. He is still working out His will in our lives. God has not forgotten us. He just has His own timetable.

A number of bad decisions—and the unpleasant consequences that went with them—have made me much more aware of the need for patience. Again, there is so much unavoidable pain in this life that I want to avoid all the avoidable pain I can.

And one way of doing that is to be patient, to be willing to give up my immediate desires for the sake of higher long-term goals.

Look down the road. Master your emotions. Listen to counsel. Get a grip on truth and do the right thing—the thing that is right in the long run, not the short run.

Life-Check

1. What experience can you remember in which you were impatient and made an emotional decision that you ended up regretting?

2. What experience have you seen in other people's lives in which they have made a rash decision that turned out badly?

3. What situation are you facing right now in which you could be in danger of losing patience and making an emotional decision that you might regret later? What can you do to make sure you make a good decision?

For Further Reflection

Scripture

Proverbs 15:14
1 Corinthians 9:24-27
2 Corinthians 4:16-18
Colossians 3:1-3

Books

Emotions: Can You Trust Them, James Dobson
30 Days to Understanding How To Live as a Christian, Max Anders

15

The Law of Chastity:
Skip the Pain

*Sexual purity, like a great fortress, builds a wall
of protection around both body and soul.*

Or do you not know that your body is the
temple of the Holy Spirit who is in you,
whom you have from God, and you are not
your own? For you were bought at a
price; therefore glorify God in your body.
1 Corinthians 6:19-20

*A*number of years ago I learned that John, a man I know, was getting a divorce. I was stunned. John was a pastor. I was a pastor. How could this be? His wife was lovely, and they had adorable children. And now he was running away with someone in the church. I was shocked.

God does not forbid sexual sin because He wants to deprive or limit us. Rather, it is because He wants to protect and fulfill us.

I don't know what John *thought* was going to happen, but what *really* happened is that his life fell apart, his wife's life fell apart, and his kids' lives fell apart. Did he think it was going to be a never-ending summer? That only happens in the movies. Last I heard he was eking out a miserable living, doing something he hated.

What causes this to happen? What short circuit of logic and reason happens to cause these astonishing moral lapses, these collapses of Christian behavior? Why is sexual sin so epidemic, and why are Christians so vulnerable?

I read in a Christian magazine a while back this stunning admission by an anonymous pastor:

> My sin of adultery had its roots in a fantasy life I had nurtured since my teenage years. As a boy, I always felt guilty whenever I looked at *Penthouse* or made a trip to the adult bookstore. Little did I know then that my obsession with pornography would one day contribute to my becoming emotionally and physically involved with a woman who was not my wife.
>
> I knew the relationship was wrong, but other than prayer, I never really sought any help. I wish I had. Each time I succumbed to sin,

I experienced extreme guilt and asked God to forgive me. But I kept on doing the wrong. Finally, I got to the point where I could no longer handle my double life. So I repented again (this time sincerely), cut off the relationship, and renewed my commitment to God and my wife. During a personal retreat time, I prayed and fasted and experienced God's forgiveness and renewal.[1]

He goes on to explain how the Lord rebuilt his shattered world (*Rebuilding Your Broken World* by Gordon McDonald was very helpful to him).

In the same magazine was this confession from a homemaker:

I am a Christian wife and mother, and I had an affair. I was forced to deal with my sin and its consequences because I became pregnant. At first, I tried to ignore the consequences, but the guilt became overwhelming. I was overcome by the reality of my situation: I was powerless over my addiction to sexual sin. I was playing games with real people whom I loved. I was living a lie by bringing another man's child into my marriage. And I was totally incapable of fixing the mess I was in.

I was a very broken woman when I crawled back to the loving arms of my heavenly Father and asked for forgiveness, mercy, and wisdom. My Father met me where I was and restored me to Himself. It was very painful to confront my husband, pastor, and church with the truth. God forgives in an instant, but the people in my world are human and needed more time. They were very hurt by what I had done and each one had to forgive at his or her own pace.

My husband and I have picked up the pieces and gone on with our lives. We are happy and know that it is by God's grace that our marriage was saved.[2]

Many years ago, when I first became a Christian, this subject would never have been a feature article. Today sexual sin is a fact in the church in America, not only among the sheep but also among the shepherds.

The sexual revolution that began in the sixties has broken lives and brought catastrophe after catastrophe to countless numbers in America, and it threatens to unravel the basic fabric of American society.

In a chapter on chastity, a thousand things could be said about this foundational Christian virtue, but the single issue I want to highlight is the fact that God does not forbid sexual sin because He wants to deprive or limit us. Rather, it is because He wants to protect and fulfill us. God is not up in heaven shouting "No!" to everything we enjoy. Rather, He tells us what we can enjoy without pain, and what will bring pain. He has not only His own honor but our good in mind.

How does God decide what is good for us and what isn't? What are His criteria? Things that reflect the character of God are good. Things that depart from His character are bad. God has created us in His image, and "one man with one woman for life" is part of the fulfillment of His image in us.

When we deviate from the character of God, we get God's opposite. God is holy, loving, good, joyful, and kind. The opposite of God is unholy, hateful, bad, painful, and cruel. Sin is any departure from the character of God, and it always brings pain. Sexual sin brings some of the greatest pain that a human being can experience. Because God doesn't want us to experience that kind of pain, He warns us against it, and we ignore His warning to our own peril.

The Bible is clear about human sexuality. We don't have to debate it or vote. The sexual revolution has not ushered in a new morality. It is still the same old immorality. It has been around since the beginning of time. The Bible says "flee sexual immorality" (1 Cor. 6:18), run from all forms of immorality (Eph. 5:3), avoid adultery (Eph. 5:5). Don't even think about it (Matt. 5:28).

Things that reflect the character of God are good. Things that depart from His character are bad.

I believe that Christians are looking for reasons to be pure and the strength to be pure. It should be enough to know that God wants us to be sexually pure. However, beyond that formidable and sufficient reason, there are several others.

What is the physical price of sexual sin?
The physical price of sexual sin is sexually transmitted disease.

It is madness to be sexually promiscuous today. With the prevalence of sexually transmitted diseases, it's like playing Russian roulette. Billy Graham told the story during one of his televised crusades of a movie star who picked up a prostitute on the streets of Hollywood and went to a nearby hotel. After engaging in sexual acts with him, the prostitute went into the bathroom and did not come out for some time. The movie star went in to see what happened. She had left through the bathroom window, and in lipstick she had written on the mirror, "Welcome to the world of AIDS."

Most Christians would never pick up a prostitute, but many are tempted to have sex with someone who is not their spouse. Yet the roulette game continues, because if you have sex with someone, in terms of the transmission of diseases, you're also having sex with everyone he or she has had sex with. Who knows where those people have been and what they have done? The rise in bisexualism is bringing AIDS and other diseases that used to be confined largely to the homosexual community into the heterosexual community.

There is great physical danger in illicit sex. There is no such thing as safe sex outside of "one man and one woman for life." Immoral sex can kill you.

What is the psychological price of sexual sin?
The psychological price of sexual sin is guilt, shame,
and a devastated self-esteem.

There is no such thing as free love, because someone always pays the price for promiscuity. The Bible teaches us not to be deceived, that God is not mocked. Whatever a person sows, that shall he or she also reap (Gal. 6:7).

Deep emotional wounds are inflicted with sexual sin. The

testimonies of both the pastor and the homemaker in previous pages reflect this. They couldn't handle their guilt and shame. The consuming remorse, damaged self-image, and haunting memories that often accompany sexual sin can destroy the future enjoyment of sex in marriage.

In addition, a person can become sexually addicted. Then it takes more and more to satisfy, which can lead to pornography and various perversions. Sexual sin distorts the intellect, defiles the conscience, and destroys the will.

<hr/>

What is the spiritual price of sexual sin?
The spiritual price of sexual sin is alienation from God and other Christians.

There is something intensely spiritual about sexual intimacy. British journalist G.K. Chesterton used to say that the man who knocks on the door of a brothel is knocking for God. I would add that the prostitute who works in the brothel was also looking for God, but in the wrong place.

Some proponents of the sexual revolution have tried to convince us that the sexual act is no more spiritual than a good meal or a deep-muscle massage. Yet they have been no more successful at destroying our innate realization of the spiritual nature of sexual union than the Soviet Union was at stamping out God. The thirst for God is innate and cannot be stamped out. Just so, the realization that sexual intercourse is more than a handshake is innate and cannot be stamped out.

The more we observe our society's obsession with sex, the more it seems that it is a thirst for something beyond the physical; it is a thirst for meaning, for belonging, for unity with God. The farther we get from God, the more we try to fill the void with sexual gratification. This is one of the explanations for why the United States, with a Christian heritage, is now so obsessed with sex. When we left God, the vacuum ached to be filled, and we try to fill it with sex.

Glamour magazine asked its readers "Are there are any virgins left out there?" Two thousand women wrote in to say yes, they were virgins—and proud of it. These were women who were virgins by choice. They told of being humiliated and teased and made to feel like freaks. Some women even sent in photos to prove that they were normal human beings. Almost all of them listed AIDS and sexually transmitted diseases as good reasons to remain chaste. Others said they didn't want to be pressured into sex by peers and the media.

Many said sex is too meaningful for a casual relationship. As one woman put it, "a lot of feelings, trust, and intimacy are put into a relationship once sex is involved." That's why she wants to save it for a relationship that is going to last. Others warned that sex outside marriage loses its meaning. One woman said that sex is for expressing love—and you can't possibly love a new person every few months.

These women didn't express a low view of sex. Just the opposite. They saw it as so meaningful, so special, that it should be saved for marriage. One letter-writer said, "God doesn't forbid sex before marriage because He wants to put us in a box with a list of rules and no fun. No, it's because He wants the best for us."[3]

Some proponents of the sexual revolution have tried to convince us that the sexual act is no more spiritual than a good meal or a deep-muscle massage.

Does God forgive sexual sin? Of course. He is willing to forgive all sin. But when we rebel against His Word, we invoke the discipline of God as well as the natural consequences of our sin. Yes, God will forgive us, but He will not take away the consequences. We still pay a price for our sin.

Yet while the clock cannot be turned back physically, it can be spiritually. God will forgive the repentant one, and when he or she commits to being physically pure, in the eyes of God the person becomes spiritually pure. Jesus told the woman caught in the act of adultery that because of her repentant attitude He did not condemn her (John 8:1-11). There is no need to condemn yourself if God does not condemn you.

While God's compassion is always extended to one who repents, we cannot let that compassion keep us from proclaiming the divine standard of no sex outside of marriage. That is the standard, and if you have not violated it, don't. If you have, repent, accept God's forgiveness, be cleansed and changed by God, and go forward in renewed spiritual purity.

As Christians, we must make a commitment to moral purity and holiness and godliness. We must flee illicit sex and commit ourselves to Christ. That is the only way to true and complete satisfaction, dignity, and liberty.

God has our best interests in mind.

We can forever put to rest the misconception that God is a cosmic killjoy, waiting to squash anyone having fun. There are good reasons to maintain moral purity, difficult though it may be. Billy Graham once said that his grandson must face temptations before 8:30 in the morning than he (Billy) had running around on Friday nights looking for it. Sexual temptation is everywhere. Television, movies, music, peer pressure, billboards, magazines. Like a chocaholic trying to stay slim while swimming in a vat of chocolate, so it is with us. We must remain pure though we're swimming in a vat of sexual temptation.

Nevertheless God asks us and enables us to remain morally pure. It may be extremely difficult and take the help of others, especially if you have already violated God's standards. It's hard to crawl back up the slippery slope once you have started down it. But it can be done.

Life-Check

1. How would you express in your own words the importance of sexual purity?

2. The Bible says that we are not only to avoid adultery, we are to not even think about it. If you were to fully obey that

command, how would it affect your television viewing, the movies you attend, the magazines you read, and the music you listen to?

3. Sexual purity is not a value espoused by television and movies. Do you think that TV and movie stars are immune to the penalties of sexual immorality? How much hidden pain do you think exists among celebrities? Why do you think sex has become a dominant theme throughout the media?

For Further Reflection

Scripture
Matthew 5:28
John 8:1-11
1 Corinthians 6:18-20
Galatians 6:7
Ephesians 5:3-5
1 Corinthians 6:19-20

Books
Why Wait, Josh McDowell
The Wounded Heart, Dan Allender

16

The Law of the Track Record:

A Good Reputation Is Priceless

What a person did yesterday,
he will tend to do tomorrow.

A good name is to be chosen
rather than great riches.
Proverbs 22:1

*I*saw on the news recently an exposé on a telephone scam, a fraudulent scheme for tricking people out of money. The scam artists preyed on the unsophisticated elderly. In one example the scam artist called older persons and tried to convince them that they had just won a valuable prize from a publisher's clearinghouse, a brand new Cadillac Sedan de Ville worth $45,000. All the "winners" had to do was pay the sales tax on the car and it would be delivered to them. The tax was 8 percent of $45,000, or $3,600. This was a lot of money, but nothing compared to the value of the car. So, many victims sent the checks for $3,600 and then never heard from the caller again.

> *Anyone who automatically believes what someone else says is at high risk for becoming a victim.*

Another telephone scam preyed on the insecurities of elderly people who were having trouble remembering things. The scam artist would call John Doe and say, "John, I was able to get you a piece of the action on that oil investment. It's only $10,000, like I said, but it will yield ten times that amount in one year. So get the check to me right away, and sit back and relax until I make you rich!"

Now, John didn't remember telling anybody he wanted to make an investment in an oil deal, but he was embarrassed about his forgetfulness and fearful that he was losing his mind. So out of embarrassment, he sent the check without telling anyone about it.

The scams are endless, and anyone who automatically believes what someone else says is at high risk for becoming a victim.

I have read about and seen on television other less elaborate scams, many times involving automobile repair. *Reader's Digest* and *Sixty Minutes* went into repair shops knowing the car they brought in was in good working order except for a disconnected spark plug wire which made the engine run a little rough. A minority of the shops simply reattached the wire. Many charged anywhere from twenty to hundreds of dollars for bogus repairs.

Other times we get taken in, not by dishonest people, but by unreliable people who promise more than they can deliver, or who forget, or who are simply incorrect, and they do us damage.

What is the importance of a track record?
Everyone has a track record of performance that will either enhance or detract from his credibility.

My father used to say, "Paper will hold still for anything." He meant that you can't automatically believe what you read. The same is true with spoken words. You cannot automatically believe what you hear. People can say anything, so how do we know we can believe them? They may be dishonest, unreliable, or incompetent. In any case, if we believe them, we come out the loser.

There are no guarantees in life, but perhaps the most valuable measure of the words someone speaks is his or her track record. A history of credibility and reliability in the past is the best indicator of credibility and reliability in the future. The same is true if someone has a track record of unreliability or untrustworthiness.

However, the typical American is basically honest and wants to believe that other people are basically honest. So we often take people at their word. Or we may feel sorry for a person and want to give him a second chance, even though we know he or she has a poor track record. Often in such cases, we get taken.

My wife, Margie, and I have tried a number of times to help people because we felt compassion for them. These were people who seemed to be in genuine need because of circumstances beyond their control. In almost every case the people turned out to be exceedingly skilled at manipulating others (even though in some cases it was not conscious manipulation), and we have been taken to the cleaners.

Because I have a soft heart, I now realize I must exercise greater care because in most cases I simply made it easier for people to be irresponsible. I'm confident I have given people fairly large sums of money, and they turned around and squandered it on booze or drugs or something else detrimental.

The point is, people can say anything. So our ability to trust or believe what they say is rooted primarily in their track record.

Here are some areas where a person's track record is critical.

Employment: When we have to employ someone, we ask for a résumé so we can look at the prospective employee's track record. Then, because paper *will* hold still for anything, we ask for references—people who can confirm the information on the résumé.

Purchases: When we are buying insurance or a car or clothing, what the salesman says to us has no credibility whatsoever by itself. But if you buy from someone you know or from a company that has a good reputation, there is some credibility in what a salesperson says. Again, we must consider the person's track record and reputation.

That is why I buy many of my clothes and whatever else I can at stores with a reputation for honoring their "satisfaction guaranteed" pledges. These are companies that sell quality merchandise at a fair price, and if you're ever dissatisfied with something you buy from them at any time in the life of the product, you can return it for a refund or replacement with no questions asked. Now that's a track record!

Relationships: One of the most crucial times to consider track records is when we are dating and considering marrying someone. All too often we get emotionally involved with someone and stop thinking clearly. We get so bonded to the other person that we don't think about his or her track record. We think someone as wonderful as this person is doesn't need any verification. Or sometimes we think if we marry a person, we can change him or her.

This often ends in disaster. An example I have seen over and over again in my ministry is a Christian woman who gets emotionally involved with a non-Christian man. Perhaps he had a religious experience as a child but has not lived for the Lord in many years. He decides to get interested in Christianity again because he knows it is important to the woman. Or perhaps the woman has told him that she cannot marry a non-Christian, so instead of a foxhole conversion, we get a marriage-chapel conversion.

A history of credibility and reliability in the past is the best indicator of credibility and reliability in the future.

He starts going to church and going through other motions because he wants to win the woman's affection. He professes a newfound faith. The woman trusts his words and marries him. Then, almost before the ink is dry on the marriage certificate, he reverts to his old ways. The Christian woman is often stuck in a disappointing, dead-end marriage, and in some cases an abusive relationship. (People who abuse seem to be especially good at manipulating people with words.) The one thing she wanted more than anything else in this world—a good, Christian marriage—is now lost to her. It is sad and all too common.

What can we learn from our own track record?
We can use it to face reality and allow the Lord to change us.

We all can learn one lesson from the law of a track record: We tend to do tomorrow what we did yesterday. When we evaluate our lives and see things that need changing, we must accept the reality that (1) other people know that is true about us, and it may be hurting our success in life, and (2) if we want to change, it will often take time and effort.

If we have missed promotions because we are careless in our work or if we have lost a significant other because we are demanding and perfectionistic or if we are lonely because we are unfriendly and judgmental or possessive and manipulative, we need to accept responsibility for our actions. We must not blame someone or something else. We must look at ourselves in the mirror and say, "You are the problem, and you must change." Then, over time, we can build a new track record.

We can change. That is one of the great messages of Christianity. "Christ in us" can make a difference. Our future doesn't have to be a continuation of our past. But only if we accept responsibility for our actions, repent, and cast ourselves on the Lord and ask Him to change what must be changed.

What can we learn from others' track records?
We can use it to get a better picture of reality and make better decisions about our future with that person.

The second lesson we need to learn from the law of the track record is that we cannot merely take people's word for anything that is important. We must take into account their record. If a car manufacturer makes certain claims about a car, we can check it out with *Consumer Reports* and other services. If we are considering employment with a company, we can check it out with civic organizations, previous and current employees, and other businesses. If we are visiting a new church, we can attend for a while to see if its promotional literature matches reality before we join.

Most importantly, if we are considering marrying a person, we need to ask ourselves, "What kind of a lifestyle was the person living before he met me?" because that is probably the lifestyle he or she will live after you get married. You cannot go by recent changes, and you cannot go by what the person tells you. Even though he or she may be perfectly sincere at the time, the person will usually resort to the lifestyle he or she was living before you met.

Now if you really love the person and are willing to invest some time in the relationship, then you can give the person enough time to create a new track record. That is, you can keep dating, but do so for long enough that you can be reasonably assured that the changes are going to be permanent. How long? I don't know. Each person is different, but I don't think a new track record can be credibly established in less than a year, and very likely longer.

> *The only way to overcome a poor track record is to prove that you have broken the old patterns and replaced them with good ones.*

Since a track record is the main thing that can be trusted, if we are going to make a big decision, we need to give it proper weight in our evaluation. Not to do so is to invite trouble or disaster.

Building a Strong Track Record

Every person has a track record. He has a track record in relationships, in employment, and in serving Christ. That track record is either a good one, an average one, or a poor one. Since what a person did yesterday he will tend to do tomorrow, performance is a vital issue in assessing future performance. It would be wrong to say a person will never change. I know I have changed and would be disappointed if people judged me today on the basis of my performance in the past. On the other hand, it would be equally unwise and naive to believe and act upon words only, rather than a demonstrated and sustained record of performance.

The only way to overcome a poor track record is to prove that you have broken the old patterns and replaced them with good ones. The same is true with someone you are evaluating. Paper will stand still for anything. People can say anything they want, and they may even be sincere. But their track record never lies.

Life-Check

1. Have you ever made bad decisions because you trusted someone's word and didn't take into account his or her track record? What insights has that experience given you about future decisions?

2. What would others say about your track record in relationships, employment, and your Christian life?

3. What changes do you think you need to make to enhance your track record?

For Further Reflection

Scripture
Proverbs 22:1
1 Thessalonians 1:6-7
1 Timothy 3:1-7

Books
The Measure of a Man, Gene Getz
The Measure of a Woman, Gene Getz

17

The Law of Contamination:
Avoiding Fleas

When you lie down with dogs,
you get up with fleas.

Can a man take fire to his bosom,
And his clothes not be burned?
Can one walk on hot coals,
And his feet not be seared?
Proverbs 6:27-28

*I*n the early days of the Wild West, there was no organized law. Unscrupulous people often did whatever they wanted, because law enforcement was inadequate to stop them. Jesse James, Billy the Kid, and the Dalton Gang became infamous as a result.

Lawlessness is a dreadful situation because the law of the jungle becomes the law of the land. Those with the power make the rules. As civilization expanded in the west, everyone breathed a sigh of relief as towns got organized, passed laws, and elected mayors and sheriffs to protect the innocent.

On the other hand, some pretty unusual laws were passed, some of which are still on the books today simply because the responsible law-making bodies never got around to eliminating them. For example, in Amarillo, Texas, it is against the law to take a bath on the main street during banking hours. In Portland, Oregon, it is illegal to wear roller skates in public rest rooms. In Halethorpe, Maryland, a kiss in public lasting more than one second is an illegal act.

Lawlessness is a dreadful situation because the law of the jungle becomes the law of the land.

These laws seem silly now. But it is easy to see that both extremes—too few laws and too many laws—should be avoided.

So it is with Christianity. From the first days of Christianity, the church has struggled with the two extremes—having too many laws on the one hand and having too few on the other. It is like riding a bicycle across a tightwire high above a circus floor. You don't want to fall to the right any more than you want to fall to the left. The Christian must keep his balance between

---

166

legalism (too many laws) and license (too few laws). In the middle is authentic Christianity.

In addition, it is not always a matter of the number of laws, but the spirit with which they are kept. For instance, one athlete may keep a strict regimen of training because he wants to. He longs to achieve the goal of athletic excellence and is willing to pay the price for it. Another athlete, however, might be keeping to the training regimen not because he wants to but because he feels he must in order to make his father happy. He himself hates it and is only keeping up the effort to earn the favor of someone else. A third person makes no attempt to achieve athletic excellence. In fact, he is a couch potato who abuses his body by eating poorly and never exercising. He is free from all unpleasant restrictions, though he is also unhealthy. In these three people we see imperfect examples of three approaches to Christianity: authentic Christianity, legalism, and license.

What is legalism?

Legalism is the belief that you gain and maintain acceptance with God by adhering to a set of external rules.

Legalism is difficult to define for a couple of reasons. First, the term is not used consistently. Second, it is a matter of attitude as much as actions. Like the athletes we saw above, two people might do the same thing but with different motives. One might be legalistic and another authentic.

One characteristic of legalism comes from the lifestyles of the Pharisees in the New Testament. They were conservative religious leaders who established their own rules for living and said that in order to be acceptable to God, you had to keep their man-made rules as well as those written in the Scripture. In fact, in the most extreme examples, they even violated Scripture in order to keep their man-made rules (Mark 7:6-13).

For example, the Pharisees had a ceremonial washing of hands that they observed before eating a meal, and they considered it a sin not to practice this ceremony. There is nothing in the Bible about it, but they drew, by inference, certain things out of the Bible and endowed the restrictions with the same weight as the Scripture.

Another characteristic of legalism is separation from the world. The central passage for this is 2 Corinthians 6:14-17:

> Do not be unequally yoked together with unbelievers. For what fellowship has righteousness with lawlessness? And what communion has light with darkness? And what accord has Christ with Belial? Or what part has a believer with an unbeliever? And what agreement has the temple of God with idols? For you are the temple of the living God. As God has said:
>
> > "I will dwell in them
> > And walk among them.
> > I will be their God,
> > And they shall be My people."
> > Therefore
> > "Come out from among them
> > And be separate, says the Lord.
> > Do not touch what is unclean,
> > And I will receive you."

The idea inherent in the passage, of course, is valid: We are not to practice the sinful things that godless people practice. However, legalists tend to go beyond what Scripture teaches and give equal weight to both cultural obligations and Scripture.

In addition, legalism tends to focus only on external sins, not internal ones. Church catechisms and biblical instruction often mention two types of sin: omission and commission. Sins of omission are good things you should have done but didn't. Sins of commission are sins you committed but shouldn't have. Legalists tend to focus on sins of commission, that is, things you shouldn't do. The traditional list includes readily identifiable things such as drinking, smoking, gambling, dancing, going to movies, and other "worldly entertainment." Rarely do they focus on sins of omission rooted in pride, lack of love, or anger.

Legalism has abounded in the American church in years past. When I was a new Christian in the 1960s, many people I associated with said you could not smoke, drink, play cards, go to dances, go to movies, wear long hair or beards, or fraternize with non-Christians. (The joke in our college was, "We don't smoke or drink or chew; and we don't go with girls [or boys] who do.") Granted, there were problems with some of these things, but legalists tend to have a knee-jerk reaction to them. Rather than appeal to a smoker, for example, that he ought not to smoke because it is dangerous to his health and dishonoring to the human body and therefore to God, the legalist may simply denounce the smoker as a calloused sinner and rebuke him for being rebellious or carnal.

What is license?

License is the attitude that we can do whatever we want because we are "free in Christ."

The days of widespread legalism seem largely gone. In many churches, legalism has been replaced with a free-for-all, if-it-feels-good-do-it, judge-not-lest-ye-be-judged mentality. Many Christians have thrown off prudent restraints in favor of being free to do whatever is not strictly forbidden. The mind-set of many people is that a Christian is free to do anything if he is not personally convicted that it is wrong, regardless of godly counsel or wise safeguards. Favorite verses are 1 Corinthians 4:3, "But with me it is a very small thing that I should be judged by you or by a human court. In fact, I do not even judge myself." Another favorite is Titus 1:15, "To the pure all things are pure."

They see no need to allow their faith to govern all the areas of their lives. They compartmentalize their faith, claiming to love God and follow Christ in religious things, but not allowing Scripture to govern other areas of their lives.

In more extreme examples, some even feel free to do things expressly forbidden in the Bible, under the provision that God forgives our sins. It is easier to get forgiveness than permission, so sin now and repent later is their logic.

———◆———

What is authentic Christianity?
*Authentic Christianity steers a prudent course
between legalism and license.*

Scripture warns us to steer a course between these two extremes. Legalism says, "If I keep this list of do's and don'ts, I am all right with God and my fellow man." License says, "I can do whatever I choose. I'm free in Christ." Authentic Christianity says, "I will do this and not do that because I love God and want to please Him and do what is best for Him, for me, and for the others whose lives I impact."

If we are going to live lives of balanced, responsible, authentic Christianity, we must accept accountability for our attitudes and actions, whether they are legalistic or licentious. The legalists need to lighten up and accept that in morally neutral matters, they cannot impose their own convictions on others.

> *As Christians in America, we have
> lain down with some of the dogs
> of this permissive world, and we
> have gotten up with the fleas of
> personal and corporate sin.*

In his book *The Grace Awakening*, Charles Swindoll tells the story of a young couple who came back from the mission field because they were ostracized by the other missionaries they worked with. The reason? The young couple had made arrangements for friends from the states to regularly send them peanut butter, which was not available on the mission field. The other missionaries disapproved of their "indulgence" and snubbed them so soundly that it broke their resolve to stay on the mission field.[1] It sounds petty, but all legalism does when the light of truth is shined on it.

On the other hand, tolerant Christians must realize that

God's commands need to be taken seriously and that not everything we should or shouldn't do is spelled out in the Bible. Common sense can take us beyond the specific words of Scripture. For example, the Bible doesn't talk specifically about abortion, but you can put two and two together and see God is against it.

Charles Colson, in his book *Faith on the Line*, tells of a conversation he had with a CBS executive during which Colson chided the executive for not airing more wholesome programming. The executive told him that CBS aired *Chariots of Fire*, a movie that presented Christians in a favorable light. The same evening, the other two networks aired *On Golden Pond* and *My Mother's Secret Life*—a soap opera about a mother who was hiding her past as a prostitute. The other two movies did very well in the ratings. CBS was clobbered. The executive asked Colson where all his wholesome Christian viewers were that evening. Colson had no answer.[2]

If Christians were watching *My Mother's Secret Life*, they were peeping into the sordid world of prostitution, entertaining themselves with things that were not proper for them (Ps. 101:2-3, Eph. 5:11-12, Phil. 4:8).

Legalism and license will always be with us, but since the mid-1960s, license is becoming the greater problem. We live in a permissive age, and cultural permissiveness has had its influence on the church.

There is an old proverb: "If you lie down with dogs, you will get up with fleas." As Christians in America, we have lain down with some of the dogs of this permissive world, and we have gotten up with the fleas of personal and corporate sin.

What modern "dogs" are giving us fleas?
There are many, but perhaps the most influential are the modern media.

Studies of different diets around the world confirm the proverb. We *are* what we eat. As that is true physically, it is also true spiritually. We become what we allow into our minds.

Television, movies, music, and magazines celebrate sex, violence, blasphemy, vulgarity, and self-centeredness. So it should come as no surprise to us that if we mentally feed on these things, we will become like them. Yet many Christians are not as cautious as they should be about avoiding such things. These modern media are largely a moral and intellectual wasteland with several harmful effects.

First, they teach us to view the world without God. Prayer, the providence of God, the will of God, and the truth of Scripture are almost never presented as part of a legitimate worldview. Therefore, the accumulative weight of years of television teaches us to view the world and our problems, as well as potential solutions, without God.

Second, values are caught the same way we catch measles—by being around those who have them. It is impossible to watch a lot of television and not be influenced by its values. Like the frog brought to a slow boil in water, Christians have slowly allowed their values to erode, accepting as normal those attitudes and values that would have been shocking just a few years ago.

The prudent Christian must think twice about exposing himself to those things that take him in the opposite direction of his life values and goals.

Third, TV and other media consume our time and keep us from thinking about loftier things and from praying and spending time with God. It shrinks our intellectual and spiritual capacity.

For these and other valid reasons, the prudent Christian must think twice about exposing himself to those things that take him in the opposite direction of his life values and goals.

Several years ago when I was pastoring in Texas, a church member said I needed to start listening to country and western music to become a real Texan. I thought, *Listen to country and western music? Why would I want to do that?* The country and western music I have listened to, with rare exceptions, deals with marital infidelity, sexual promiscuity, alcohol abuse, brooding and other morose emotional behavior, and irresponsible living. (Someone once asked me, "Do you know what you get if you play country and western music backward?" I said I had no idea. He said, "You get your wife back, you get your job back, you get your house back, you get your truck back, you get your dog back, you get your . . .") Why would I want to listen to something that erodes my own values?

Country and western music is not the only problem. What about rock and rap with their violence, sensuality, and drug-related overtones? A less obvious problem is popular or easy-listening music. What happens to our moral edge when we regularly listen to Englebert Humperdink, who sings of wanting a girl to make believe she loves him one more time, for the good times? Or when we listen to Willie and Julio singing their hearts out to all the girls they've loved before?

You must guard yourself against the media if you would keep your spiritual edge.

Just as you are what you eat, so you become what you think about. And if you feed indiscriminately on modern media, you will impede your progress toward spiritual maturity. It's not that we have a hard time understanding this or even believing it. Rather, it is that we like our television and movies and music and don't want to give them up.

Let me state the issue perfectly clearly. I have seen so many lives crippled or destroyed because people, swayed by media, violated simple and clear principles in Scripture that, had they been obeyed, could have prevented the pain. It grieves me to see the shipwrecks of so many human beings.

I ponder how these people got in the problems they are in. There are many answers, including dysfunctional homes; physical, sexual, or emotional abuse (not always originating in the home); a bad church experience; bad friends; and alcohol or drug abuse. People with these experiences often ignore or don't know biblical truth and fall into terrible problems as a result.

But there is one other thing that needs to be included in that list of harmful influences—the media. Many Christians have been so affected by modern media that their knowledge of and hunger for spiritual truth are greatly diminished. Perhaps no influence in American culture (except for a godly Christian home) is greater in establishing life values than the media, whose values are predominately anti-Christian. Therefore, if we entertain ourselves carelessly with the media, we diminish our own spiritual capacity.

I was once in a conversation with a number of people who were talking with a national Christian leader. Someone asked him what he thought was the greatest problem in the church today. Without hesitating, he said, "Carnality" (a greater desire for pleasure than for spiritual maturity). I took note of that answer. A couple of years later I was in another conversation with some people talking with a different national Christian leader, and coincidentally, he was asked the same question. Without hesitating, he said, "Carnality." It was like an instant replay, only it was two different people in two different locations at two different times.

I am personally persuaded that the cause of much of the pain in the Christian world stems from carnality, and that much of the carnality stems from overexposure to the media. My call is a simple one. Break yourself from the media habit to set yourself free to grow spiritually. You'll save yourself much pain.

Life-Check

1. By temperament or upbringing, do you think your greatest personal challenge lies with being legalistic or licentious? Why?

2. Do you think Jesus would have the same viewing, listening, and reading habits that you have? In what areas are you weak? Are you in danger of being in bondage to any media (gauged by the inability to give it up)?

3. Do the friends you have and the church you go to help you

or hurt you in your pursuit of holiness? What do you think your course of action should include to gain better mastery over media?

For Further Reflection

Scripture

Proverbs 6:27-28
Matthew 5:17-20
Mark 7:6-23
2 Corinthians 6:14-17
Philippians 4:8

1 Corinthians 4:3
Titus 1:15
Psalm 101:2-3
Ephesians 5:11-12

Books

The Grace Awakening, Charles Swindoll
Rediscovering Holiness, James Packer

18

The Law of Suffering:
Pain = Gain

Life is hard, but personal pain can foster
wisdom and spiritual depth.

Count it all joy when you fall into various
trials, knowing that the testing of your faith
produces patience. But let patience have
its perfect work, that you may be perfect
and complete, lacking nothing.
James 1:2-4

*O*ne summer, my wife and I took a driving vacation to some of the most beautiful places in the United States. We crawled into our Suburban, which is like a small living room on wheels, and headed for Santa Fe, New Mexico. From there we took Interstate 25 north to Colorado Springs, Estes Park, and the Rocky Mountain National Park, to Cheyenne, Wyoming. Then we headed west to Jackson Hole and the Grand Tetons. From there we went north and saw Yellowstone in a day. That's tough to do, as Yellowstone is roughly the size of Rhode Island.

Even Old Faithful cooperated. It normally erupts about every hour or so, but it can go as long as two-and-a-half hours before erupting. We pulled off the main road that circles Yellowstone into the Old Faithful parking lot. We walked over to the geyser hole, and it blew sky-high! We took a picture, turned on our heels, and were on our way.

Then we backtracked nearly the entire distance home. We saw some amazing scenery, met some interesting people (we picked up some Australian hitchhikers in the Rocky Mountain National Park. They had fascinating stories to tell), read a bunch of books, talked a lot, did a lot of hiking in the mountains, took some great pictures, and had a wonderful time.

All was wonderful except for one thing. I had a root canal done in Colorado Springs. It was your worst dental nightmare realized. Coming out of Jackson Hole on our way home, I began to feel a mild pulse in my lower left molar that grew into a throb by the time we reached Cheyenne. The throbbing intensified into a great crescendo of pain by the time we hit Colorado Springs. We found a dentist (a diabolical sadist) who first had to find out which one of my teeth was really causing the problem (I told him twenty times) and how bad it was (it was killing me!). After shooting liquid oxygen on it, creating enough pain to qualify me for a Purple Heart, he shot me so full of Novocain that my kneecaps went to sleep. I had felt nothing but pain for two days, and then I felt nothing at all for two days.

> *A Christian must be able to stand nose-to-nose with this mind-bending truth and not blink: A good God allows His children to suffer.*

I see my dentist every six months for a cleaning and checkup. There was no hint that I would have any trouble. Why did I have to have tooth trouble while on vacation? When I look back on it, it was a little thing, but it typifies many things in life. We hurt, and we don't know why.

One of my favorite stories when I was growing up was the Disney classic *Old Yeller*, the story of a pioneer family carving out an existence on the edge of wilderness who adopt a huge "old yeller" dog after it saves their two boys from a pack of wild pigs.

The dog lives as a beloved member of the family until it once again saves their lives during an attack by a rabid wolf. In the process, Old Yeller contracts rabies himself, and the lovable, lop-eared mutt is reduced to a snarling, mindless set of slashing teeth. The son who owned Old Yeller was faced with the incomprehensible responsibility of shooting the dog that had twice saved his life.

Afterward, in a tear-jerking scene, the father comes out to console the son on the loss of his dog—a blow that the whole family felt. I'll never forget the tender words of wisdom his father gave: "Son, sometimes life just hauls off and socks you one right in the stomach, and there's no explaining it. And all you can do is hang on until you catch your breath, and then start livin' again."

How true that is. It has happened to all of us. Life hauls off and socks us one right in the stomach, and there is no explaining it. But when we stand there, immobilized by the searing pain, doubled over, mouth agape, unable to breathe spiritually or emotionally, questions flood our minds. *Why me? Why this? Why now? Does God care? Where is God when it hurts?*

A Christian must be able to stand nose-to-nose with this mind-bending truth and not blink: A good God allows His children to suffer. Period. We can discuss the reasons. We can ponder the consequences. We can debate the rationale. We can weep in the middle of our agony. But the two towering truths remain unchanged. God is good, and His children suffer.

Though we may never fully understand why, the road to transformation always goes through the tunnel of trials. If you are on a road that does not include trials, it is not the road to transformation. God wants us to be changed into the character likeness of Christ, so He allows pain to come into our lives, then He uses that pain to make us more like His Son.

The central passage in all the Scripture on this theme is James 1:2-4, where we read:

> Count it all joy when you fall into various trials, knowing that the testing of your faith produces patience. But let patience have its perfect work, that you may be perfect and complete, lacking nothing.

From this passage, we get answers to three key questions about trials.

Who experiences trials?
Trials are unavoidable; they come to everyone.

There is no use crying "Why me?" Trials happen to all of us, if not now then later. James said count it all joy *when*, not *if*, trials come your way. However, our knee-jerk reaction is almost always, "Why me?"

I once heard the story of a man who was on his way home from work on the subway. He was prone to motion sickness, he had eaten a big lunch that didn't agree with him, he had worked hard all afternoon in a smoke-filled conference room, and he boarded the subway with an upset stomach. He was jammed into the train, the last one to get on, and the automatic door closed right at the end of his nose. He stood there, facing out the windows of the closed doors, things flashing by at ninety miles an hour, and the longer he stood there, the sicker he got.

The train pulled up to the next stop, but he did not want to get off. However, the train was so full, no one could get on, even though a small crowd was pressed near the slowing train. The lurching and jerking of the stopping train was the last straw. The door opened, and up came his lunch, all over the man waiting on the platform. The door closed without anyone getting on or off, and the train sped on down the track. The unfortunate man whose chest had become the depository for the sick man's lunch turned to the person standing next to him, raised his palms to the heavens, and cried, "Why me?"

Sooner or later, the doors of life open, and someone's lunch is deposited on our chest, and we cry, "Why me?" James answers the question. It is not just you. It is everyone. If not now, then later, but everyone. No one escapes the motion sickness of life.

What value is there in trials?
Trials make us spiritually strong.

James said, "Count it all joy . . . knowing that the testing of your faith produces patience." The Greek word for "testing" is *peirazein*. It does not imply moral temptation, as the King James Bible might be misunderstood to say, but rather, a test designed to validate or refine the finished product.

> *While God does not cause all trials,*
> *He will use them to give us endurance.*

When gold is dug out of the hills, it is mixed with clay, iron ore, mineral deposits, and other impurities. To purify the gold, all the ore is put into huge vats and heated in a furnace to a white-hot temperature until the whole mess bubbles like oatmeal. Gold is heavy, so in this liquefied state all the gold settles to the bottom and everything that is not gold rises to the top, like ugly froth. This stuff is called *dross*. The dross is skimmed off, and what is left behind is pure gold.

Just as without the heat there would be no separation of the gold from the impurities, so without trials there is often little separation of us from our personal impurities. This is the process the writer of the hymn "How Firm a Foundation" was referring to when he wrote:

When through fiery trials thy pathway shall lie,
My grace, all sufficient, shall be thy supply;
The flame shall not hurt thee; I only design
Thy dross to consume and thy gold to refine.

While God does not cause all trials, He will use them to give us endurance. The word for endurance is *hupomoné*, which means "to remain under." In his commentary on the book of James, Spiros Zodhiates writes:

Have you ever seen a blacksmith work with a piece of iron? He holds it in the fire to soften it up and make it pliable. That is exactly why God permits the testing of our faith by trials. He wants us to acquire patience, to acquire pliability. If you and I are constantly out of the fire of affliction, we become stiff and useless. God wants to reshape us according to His image, for in the fall of Adam we lost our divine image or divine shape.[1]

What is the end result of trials?
Trials can change us into the character image of Christ.

The one who is *hupomoné* remains under refinement in God's fire until God's work in him is done. Then we are "perfect and complete, lacking in nothing." If we are to become all that God wants us to become as a result of being in the fire of affliction, we must lean into the pain, remain spiritually sensitive, obedient, faithful. Whatever the test, it must be endured God's way.

Perfect does not mean without flaw. We can't become flawless human beings. Rather, *perfect* comes from the word *teleios,* which means "complete, mature, fully developed." It means we become mature in our character. "Complete" carries with it the idea of being whole. "Lacking in nothing," then, would have the idea of not being void of any major character qualities.

What pain are you facing? Is it a difficult marriage, disappointing family relationships, financial difficulties, physical pain, emotional turmoil, moral temptations, anxiety about the future? We can bolt from the ranks if we choose and squirm out of God's fire if we have the option. Or we can refuse to be softened, even though we are forced by circumstances to remain in the fire. If we fail to go through it God's way, we hurt twice. We hurt because of the trial, and we hurt because we don't gain the character development that would make life easier in the future.

There have surely been times in the life of any Christian who has suffered to a moderate or severe extent when the grace of God did not seem sufficient to bear the suffering. We think of the apostle Paul who was plagued by what he called a "thorn in the flesh" (2 Cor. 12:7-9). He prayed to the Lord three times that the thorn might be removed from him, but the Lord said to him, "My grace is sufficient for you, for My strength is made perfect in weakness."

The grace of God doesn't always enable us to go water skiing through life. Sometimes it just keeps our nostrils above the surface of the water.

Yet in some cases Christians experience what goes beyond weakness to profound suffering. It is at those times when we are perfectly willing to believe that God has a purpose in it, we just want to know how to survive. Even Jesus Himself experienced suffering that seemed to take Him beyond a calm peace. He was deeply grieved and distressed in the Garden of Gethsemane before His betrayal and crucifixion. He said to His disciples, "My soul is exceedingly sorrowful, even to death. Stay here and watch with Me." Matthew 26 tells us He then went a little beyond them "and fell on His face, and prayed" (vv. 37-39).

Luke records that "being in agony, He prayed more earnestly. Then His sweat became like great drops of blood falling down to the ground" (Luke 22:44). Later, on the cross, Jesus cried, "My God, My God, why have You forsaken Me?" (Matt. 27:46).

We see then that even in the life of our Lord, suffering was real, and the grace of God did not take away the pain. Nor did the grace of God make it a piece of cake to endure. But the grace of God did make the suffering (just barely) endurable.

In the middle of suffering, many of us would say that the grace of God did not seem sufficient. But when we look back, we see that somehow He sustained us. The grace of God doesn't always enable us to go water skiing through life. Sometimes it just keeps our nostrils above the surface of the water most of the time.

Offer your suffering to God.

There are times when the best way of dealing with our suffering is to offer our suffering to God as an act of worship. Terry Waite, emissary to the Archbishop of Canterbury, went to the Middle East to try to negotiate the release of some hostages who had been taken by some terrorists, and ended up a hostage himself. He was released at the end of 1991 after nearly five years of solitary confinement (which prison officials recognize as the worst kind of torture for most people) in Lebanon, chained to the wall of his room for almost twenty-four hours daily. After his release, he said:

> I have been determined in captivity, and still am determined, to convert this experience into something that will be useful and good for other people. I think that's the way to approach suffering. It seems to me that Christianity doesn't in any way lessen suffering. What it does is enable you to take it, face it, to work through it, and eventually to convert it.[2]

Daniel Defoe wrote in *Robinson Crusoe*, a book that many Christians are astonished to discover is filled with deep spiritual insights, that "God will often deliver us in a manner that seems, initially, to being about our destruction." It is usually only after we think we have been destroyed and survived that we begin to believe this and draw spiritual strength from its profound truth.

In a more elaborate expression, John Newton, the author of

the well-known hymn "Amazing Grace," wrote in an untitled poem:

I asked the Lord that I might grow
In faith, and love, and every grace,
Might more of his salvation know
And seek more earnestly his face.

'Twas he who taught me thus to pray,
And he, I trust, has answered prayer;
But it has been in such a way
As almost drove me to despair.

I hoped that in some favored hour
At once he'd answer my request,
And by his love's constraining power
Subdue my sins, and give me rest.

Instead of this, he made me feel
The hidden evil of my heart,
And let the angry powers of hell
Assault my soul in every part.

Yea, more, with his own hand he seemed
Intent to aggravate my woe,
Crossed all the fair designs I schemed,
Blasted my gourds, and laid me low.

"Lord, why this?" I trembling cried,
"Wilt Thou pursue thy worm to death?"
"Tis in this way," the Lord replied,
"I answer prayer for grace and faith."

"These inward trials I employ
From self and pride to set thee free,
And break thy schemes of earthly joy,
That thou mayest seek thy all in me."

The way to deal with suffering in any form—from the mildest irritation to the mental and physical agony that so absorbs and overwhelms you that you groan and scream—is to offer it to the God who has permitted it, telling Him to make what He wills of it, and of us through it. The Father sanctifies our suffering for the ripening and refining of our Christian character, for a demonstration in us of the reality of supernatural empowering, and for our actual fruitfulness in serving others. One aspect of Jesus' holiness was His willingness to suffer all kinds of pain for His Father's glory and others' good. One facet of holiness in Jesus' disciples is willingness to be led along a parallel path. . . . "Mature . . . Oh, . . . yes, I see. And I am a silly child who stumbles and fumbles and tumbles every day. Holy Father, Holy Son, Holy Spirit, I need your help. Lord, have mercy; hold me up, and hold me steady—please, starting now. Amen."[3]

I read James Packer's book *Rediscovering Holiness* during a personal time of great physical suffering. I didn't feel like I was going through it very well. The grace of God didn't seem sufficient.

Day after day, week after week, month after month, I pleaded with God to bring me relief from my suffering, to make His grace sufficient for me. Each night, I prayed that God would make tomorrow a better day. And for months at a time, tomorrow was no better; it was often worse.

In the midst of our pain, we must remind ourselves, God has not abandoned me.

I did not feel, on many occasions, that even my nostrils were above the surface. But by some miracle of grace that I can only see looking backward, I have come to see what Packer writes is indeed true. We offer our suffering to God as an act of worship to Him, knowing that He suffered more for us than we are suffering for Him. And what's more, Jesus' suffering was caused by my sin, and He willingly endured it.

The hottest fire produces the strongest steel. The wildest winds make the toughest trees. The greatest trials create the strongest faith. Wanting to be a mature Christian without significant suffering is like wanting to be the greatest athlete without training, the purest gold without refining, the finest pianist without the practice.

Certainly, if the suffering is significant, we will want to escape.

If the trial is not something that makes us cry for escape, then it is not intense enough to strengthen the steel, toughen the tree, condition the athlete, or prepare the pianist.

There is no embarrassment in wanting to escape; even Jesus wanted to escape. But often we can't. Then, in the midst of our pain, we must remind ourselves, *God has not abandoned me. This will bring about for me the deepest longings of my soul.* When you are crying for release is when you're most fitted by God for great character and service. When the pain seems unbearable, we cry out to God as Jesus did for the grace to bear the unbearable. We take hope in the fact that the sacred moment will produce great spiritual growth and great eternal reward.

Suffering is a calling for each Christian, one that prepares us for glory with Christ by drawing us deeper into the sanctity of being like Him. But we fulfill our vocation imperfectly. If someone the stature of Packer can say, "I am a silly child who stumbles and fumbles and tumbles every day," then we need not despair if we stumble and fumble and tumble. So let us pray along with him: "Holy Father, Holy Son, Holy Spirit, I need your help. Lord, have mercy; hold me up, and hold me steady—please, starting now. Amen."

Life-Check

1. What trial are you experiencing now that is at the top of your trial list? Have you prayed for insight into why you are experiencing the trial? Have you gained the insight you want?

2. If it is true that "God will often deliver us in a manner that seems, initially, to bring about our destruction," do you have a memory of a time when you thought you were being destroyed but were actually being delivered? Can you transfer the insight you gained from that experience to the number one trial you are facing today?

3. What is the greatest area of spiritual strength you need in life? What are some ways you can see how your biggest trial will give you that kind of strength?

4. What spiritual insight and ministry do you think you will be able to share with others as a result of this trial?

For Further Reflection

Scripture

1 Corinthians 10:13
2 Corinthians 1:8-10
James 1:2-4
1 Peter 1:6-9
1 Peter 4:12-16
2 Corinthians 12:7-9
Matthew 26:37-39
Matthew 27:46
Luke 22:44

Books

Rediscovering Holiness, James Packer
The Power of Suffering, John MacArthur

19

The Law of Facts:
Set Free by the Truth

Truth is true, no matter what
you think, believe, or feel.

You shall know the truth, and the
truth shall make you free.
John 8:32

I read one time of a liar's club in Burlington, Wisconsin, that you could join for one dollar and a good-enough lie. Some of the stories people used to get into the liar's club were doozies! One man said his wife's feet were so cold that every time she took her shoes off the furnace kicked on. Another man said he was fishing one day where the fish were biting so well he had to stand behind a tree to bait his hook. Someone else said he cut a tree down on a day when it was so foggy the tree didn't fall over until the fog lifted. One farmer said his wife was so lazy she fed the chickens popcorn so the eggs would turn themselves over when she was frying them.

A gentleman from Alabama looked over the national registry of the liar's club and discovered there were liars from every state in the Union except Alabama. He wrote to the liar's club, made this observation, and then added that was because there *were* no liars in Alabama. The liar's club was so deeply impressed they gave him a free lifetime membership.

These aren't really lies, of course. They are tall tales. The difference is that no one is supposed to know a lie is a lie, but *everyone* knows that a tall tale is not true. Lying is wrong. Tall tales are just good fun.

Truth needs to dominate a person's life and a society.

Sometimes real life creates some tall tales. I remember when *Life* magazine did a feature article on Robert and Elizabeth Dole, the ultimate Washington, D.C. couple. At the time Robert Dole was Senator from Kansas and Elizabeth was Transportation Secretary in the Reagan Administration. Along with the article there were a number of pictures to help people see the kind of life this unusual couple lived.

One of the pictures was of Robert and Elizabeth making the bed together one morning before leaving to go to work. An irate constituent of Robert Dole's wrote to him and said he ought to be ashamed of letting a picture be taken of him doing women's work. Dole replied, "Listen, buddy. You don't know the half of it. The only reason she was helping me was that the photographer was there!"

Other times life sounds like a tall tale, but isn't. I once heard a story reportedly involving Beverly Sills, one of our great sopranos who sang for so many years with the Metropolitan Opera. Supposedly, she said when she was first trying to break into the world of opera, she got a job traveling to remote rural areas of the United States bringing culture to places that would otherwise be unable to have it. She was scheduled to go to a very small town in the middle of nowhere in Nebraska, where, coincidentally, they were having a serious outbreak of a cattle disease called *stinking smut*. On the front page of the local paper, they got the pictures and the captions mixed up. Beneath the picture of a sick cow was the caption, "Beverly Sills to sing locally." Beneath the picture of Beverly Sills was the caption, "Stinking smut hits Nebraska!"

While outrageous stories and tall tales are harmless, lies are *very* harmful. Truth needs to dominate a person's life *and* a society. If it doesn't, darkness descends and a deep cold settles over everything. Someone once said, "When truth recedes, tyranny advances." This is true on a personal level as well as a social one.

⫷⬥⫸

Why is truth important?
Absolute truth exists whether we know the truth or not; therefore, life is dangerous unless we know what is true.

The obvious reason truth is important is that we need to know how to have eternal life. If we reject absolute truth, we reject the truth of the Bible and jeopardize our eternal destiny.

Beyond that supreme truth, there is the matter of living our daily lives. We are living in a day when the Samson of *relativism* is pushing hard on the pillars of truth and threatening to bring the house down. *Relativism* is the belief that all truth is relative.

Alan Bloom, in his masterful work *The Closing of the American Mind,* states that the single most agreed-upon truth on the American campus today is that truth is relative. That is, there is no such thing as absolute truth. Rather, each person is free to determine what is true for himself. You may believe one thing is true, and I believe the opposite, but that's okay because each thing is true to the one who believes it.[1]

This perspective is wreaking havoc with business, with our educational system, with government, the family, morals and values, and everything else in American life. As a result of it, "everyone did what was right in his own eyes" (Judges 21:25). When everyone does what is right in his own eyes, social structure begins to break down.

When we reject absolute truth,
what happens to the Bible?
The Bible becomes merely another book, not a reliable guide for this life or the next.

If we abandon the belief that absolute truth exists, we destroy the credibility of the Bible. The Bible not only declares that absolute truth exists, it claims to be absolutely true itself, down to the last single letter. If you deny the existence of absolute truth, you deny the truth of the Bible and everything it teaches.

If the Bible is wrong in its claim to be absolutely true, how can we trust it to be true in anything it says? If the Bible has one mistake in it, who's to say it doesn't have two or two hundred?

What do we lose when we lose absolute truth? We lose the Bible and all that it teaches about God, Jesus, life and death, heaven and hell. We lose hope for life after death.

When we reject absolute truth, what

happens to social stability?
Social order begins to disintegrate when we
abandon absolute truth.

Our society is sick because we are drinking from a polluted water supply of truth. Into that water supply has been dumped lies, inaccuracies, misconceptions, runaway individualism, the demand of rights without responsibilities, selfishness, sensuality, and a conviction that my happiness is more important than yours. And, as we drink from this polluted water supply, we are becoming morally ill, just as we would become physically ill if we were drinking real water from a reservoir containing filth, waste, and disease.

Truth is what God says it is, regardless
of what we believe or what we feel.

I am persuaded that the reason many people do not believe in absolute truth is because they are free from moral obligations imposed by society and don't want God putting any back on them. They like their freedom. But they are like the dog who has broken his chain and thinks he is free, only to run out into the street and get hit by a car.

We may have little influence over the world's values, but we have great influence over the church's values, and there we must raise the call for absolute truth. Truth is what God says it is, regardless of what we believe or what we feel.

When we reject absolute truth, what

happens to right and wrong?
If there is no absolute truth, there is no
such thing as right and wrong.

As Dostoyevsky wrote in *The Brothers Karamazov*, "If there is no God, then all things are permissible." Do you believe the holocaust was wrong? Why? Hitler thought it was right. Do you believe child pornography is wrong? Why? The pornographers think it is right. Do you think rape is wrong? Why? The rapist thinks it is right. If you cannot appeal to an authority higher than humanity, you cannot say that something another person does is wrong.

The world is a frightening place without God and the Bible. Attila the Hun, Genghis Khan, Nero, Adolph Hitler, Stalin, Idi Amin, Pol Pot, and a thousand nameless monsters throughout history are the legacy of mankind ruling others without God and the Bible. Right and wrong disappear, and those with the power make the rules.

What happens when we accept absolute truth?
If we know the truth, the truth can set us free.

Jesus said, "You shall know the truth, and the truth shall make you free" (John 8:32). He also said, in a prayer to God the Father for His disciples, "Sanctify them by Your truth. Your word is truth" (John 17:17). By putting these two passages together, we see that if the truth shall set us free, and if God's Word is truth, then we will be set free by studying and following the Word of God, the Bible.

This is a stunning truth. It is so simple, its implications so dramatic, and yet it is so universally ignored, even among Christians, that it is unbelievable. I suppose it is no more unbelievable than the fact that people still smoke in spite of tobacco's link to cancer, people still drink in spite of the dangers of alcohol, and people still eat high-fat diets in spite of the link of high cholesterol to heart problems. But it is difficult to believe, nevertheless.

David said in Psalm 119: "How can a young man cleanse his way? / By taking heed according to Your word. . . . Your word I have hidden in my heart / That I might not sin against You" (vv. 9, 11).

The Lord said to Joshua:

> This Book of the Law shall not depart from your mouth, but you shall meditate in it day and night, that you may observe to do according to all that is written in it. For then you will make your way prosperous, and then you will have good success. (Josh. 1:8)

Would you like for your way to be prosperous? Would you like to have success? Then be careful to do all that is written in the Bible. That means you must meditate on it day and night. Success in life is not given as a reward, like a lollipop, for studying and memorizing and meditating on the Bible. The success comes from *doing* what the Bible says.

The *Today's English Version* has a helpful colloquial translation of this verse: "Be sure that the book of the Law is always read in your worship. Study it day and night, and make sure that you obey everything written in it. Then you will be prosperous and successful."

———————————————

What are our responsibilities to absolute truth?
If we believe we know truth, we must live it and share it.

There are three things in our lives that we must keep in proper order: facts, faith, and feelings. All three must be alive and well if we are to live lives of purpose and satisfaction. But like the engine, coal car, and caboose of a train, they must be kept in the proper order. If you get them out of order, the train won't run.

Facts are the engine. They must be first. Truth must run our lives, not faith, not feelings. If *faith* runs our lives, we may believe something that is wrong. If *feelings* run our lives, we may do something that feels good up front but hurts us down the road, like taking illegal drugs. Facts, and facts alone, have the right to lead our lives.

As Christians, our first great task is to get it right ourselves—to be sure we are not believing something that is not true. We must be serious students of the Scriptures and faithful followers of what we learn.

After that our second great task is to help others get it right. To help others see that faith is only as safe as its object, and feelings can only be trusted as they line up with the facts.

If the truth is that the person we're dating is not mature enough to sustain a marriage relationship with us, then a marriage with that person will fail, regardless of what we believe or how we feel when we are dating.

There are three things in our lives that we must keep in proper order: facts, faith, and feelings.

If the truth is that we cannot afford to buy that house we have our heart set on, we will end up in deep financial trouble regardless of what we believe or how we feel when we buy it.

If the truth is that the business deal we're putting together is dishonest, we may end up with a ruined reputation or a criminal record regardless of what we believe or how we feel when we make it.

And if the truth is that without repenting of our sins and turning to Christ for salvation, we will spend eternity separated from God, then that remains true regardless of what we believe or how we feel about it.

Whatever it might be—money, relationships, work, school, health, or our relationship with God—we had better find out what the truth is and go with it. Truth always reigns.

Combine love and the truth.

The world's people hunger for meaning, for truth, and for virtue, and often, we as Christians do not give it to them. First, we don't know the truth well enough to give a credible defense of it. Second, we give them a distortion of truth because our lives are lacking virtue. Third, we often act with anger and bitterness toward the world.

When we can make a skillful, pleasing defense of what we

believe in, and back it up with good works, we send out a wonderful message. We need to demonstrate the love of Christ to the world. The world is so hardened to the Scriptures and so confused about what is truth, that it often cannot even grasp our message, let alone accept it. But when our message comes through the love of Christ, then people tend to accept the reality of what we say.

People have different views about religion, truth, and God, but that does not make all views equally valid. One person's god is not as good as another person's god because there is objective truth, and the source of that truth is the God of the Bible. Truth is not what you think it is or what you believe it is or feel it is. Truth is true, regardless of whether you know what it is or believe it.

Life-Check

1. What experience have you had in which you denied reality, persisted in foolishness, and paid a serious price?

2. Did you learn your lesson, or are you still struggling in that area?

3. Do you agree that absolute truth exists, and that the Bible is totally true? If not, how do you determine what is true and what isn't?

4. If truth sets us free, what is an area of your life in which truth has set you free?

For Further Reflection

Scripture
Joshua 1:8
Psalm 119:9,11
John 8:32
2 Timothy 2:15
John 17:17
Judges 21:25

Books
What If Jesus Had Never Been Born, D. James Kennedy
The Bible: Embracing God's Word, Max Anders

20

The Law of Faith:
The Eyes of Faith Have 20/20 Vision

Faith is only as good as the object in
which it is placed.

Now faith is the substance of things hoped for,
the evidence of things not seen.
Hebrews 11:1

*J*ames Herriot is the pen name of a veterinarian who wrote a series of books about his life in the Yorkshire highlands of northern England. He had more than his share of unusual and even dangerous things happen to him during his life, some of them due strictly to chance and others brought on by some of his own glaring lapses in judgment.

Faith is only as safe as the thing in which it is placed.

One such lapse came when he was making his rounds in the hilly high country near his home, driving a car with bad brakes. As he neared a precipitous hill with dangerous curves in the road, he couldn't decide whether or not to chance driving down it. It was much shorter to go down the steep hill with four menacing turns, but because of his bad brakes, it was a little dangerous. To turn around and go the long way was much safer, but it meant a round trip of nearly ten miles. The place he needed to go was just at the bottom of the hill. Finally, after much deliberation, he decided to place his faith in the bad brakes. Over the hill he went, dry-mouthed and white-knuckled. It was like the whole world dropped away from him, and the road seemed nearly vertical. From there, I'll let him tell the story:

> It is surprising what speed you can attain in low gear if you have nothing else to hold you back, and as the first bend rushed up at me the little engine started a rising scream of protest. When I hit the curve, I hauled the wheel around desperately to the right, the tires spun for a second in the stones and loose soil of the verge, then we were off again.
>
> This was a longer stretch and even steeper and it was like being

on [a roller coaster], with the same feeling of lack of control over one's fate. Hurtling into the bend, the idea of turning at this speed was preposterous but it was that or straight over the edge. Terror-stricken, I closed my eyes and dragged the wheel to the left. I was sure the car would turn over, but it didn't, and once more I was on my way.

Again a yawning gradient. But as the car sped downwards, engine howling, I was aware of a curious numbness. I seemed to have reached the ultimate limits of fear and hardly noticed as we shot round the third bend. One more to go and at last the road was leveling out; my speed dropped rapidly and at the last bend I couldn't have been doing more than twenty. I had made it.

It wasn't until I was right on the final straight that I saw the sheep. Hundreds of them filling the road. A river of woolly backs lapping from the stone wall on one side of the road to the stone wall on the other side of the road. They were only yards from me, and I was still going downhill. Without hesitation I turned and drove straight into the wall.

I suppose some people would have asked me what I was doing, but not a Dales shepherd. He went quietly by without invading my privacy, but when I looked in the mirror after a few moments I could see him in the middle of the road staring back at me, his sheep temporarily forgotten.[1]

I have laughed at that story until I thought I would injure myself, probably because in smaller, less wacky ways, I have done exactly the same thing.

Blind faith is not only futile, it can be downright dangerous. Faith is only as safe as the thing in which it is placed. James Herriot put his faith in bad brakes, and it almost cost him his life.

There are people who have gotten on a plane, believing it would get them safely to their final destination, but it didn't. There are people who have put their trust in faith healers only to die of a disease. There are people who have put their life savings in a business venture, believing it would make them rich, and they lost everything. Faith by itself is worthless. Worse than worthless. It's dangerous.

God wants us to have peace, love, and joy, but in order to have them we must believe the right things. We must trust the promises of God. That's why faith cannot lead our lives. Facts must. Once we get our facts straight, we then know where to put our faith.

In Chapter 1, I quoted Blaise Pascal on the subject of happiness. I must quote it again here, because his statement is crucial to understanding not only happiness but also faith. There is a clear link between what we believe and how happy we are:

> All men seek happiness. This is without exception. Whatever different means they employ, they all tend to this end. The cause of some going to war, and of others avoiding it, is the same desire in both, attending with different views. The "will" never takes the least step but to this objective. This is the motive of every man, even of those who hang themselves.

This is a crucial thing to understand. We do what we do because we *believe* it will make us happy. We may be dead wrong, and often are, but we do it nevertheless because of what we believe. When a Christian deliberately and knowingly sins, it is a breakdown of faith. He believes that the sin will make him happier than God will. The opposite of obedience, then, is not disobedience. *The opposite of obedience is unbelief!*

Therefore it is vital for us to be alert to what we believe. First we must be sure, as we said in Chapter 1, that what we believe is rooted in facts. Second, we must be sure we actually believe what we say or think we believe.

What is faith?
Faith is believing what God has said and acting accordingly.

Some cynics have defined faith as "believing in spite of the fact that there is nothing to believe." Or worse, "believing in spite of all the evidence to the contrary." In the classic movie *Miracle on 34th Street,* Santa Claus utters what much of the world thinks faith is: "Faith is believing in things when common sense tells you not to." In other words, faith is irrational, contrary to experience, logic, and knowledge.

In the Walt Disney cartoon *Pinocchio,* Jiminy Cricket sings, "When you wish upon a star, your dreams come true." That's what faith is like for many people. It is like wishful thinking. Jiminy believed that if you wished hard enough, your dream would come true. Many people think that if they just believe hard enough, their prayers will come true. That simply isn't true. Faith in *faith* is no good. Believing is futile if you are believing something that isn't true.

When a Christian deliberately and knowingly sins, it is a breakdown of faith. He believes that the sin will make him happier than God will.

Let me offer a better definition of faith: Faith is believing what God has said and acting accordingly. It is fruitless to pray for everyone in the whole world to be saved, because the Bible has made it clear that the whole world will not be saved. Faith must be tied to truth. It is futile to believe that all the problems in your life will be resolved the way you want them to be resolved, because the Bible makes it clear that won't happen. It is futile to believe we will get everything we ask God for. Scripture makes it clear we won't. That's why facts must lead our lives, not faith. It is only as we know the facts that we know what to put our faith in.

For example, the Federal Aviation Administration (FAA) recently said that a certain type of propeller-driven commuter airplane could no longer fly in conditions in which icing was likely to occur. Several crashes of that type airplane had occurred during icing conditions. If you know that kind of plane tends to crash when ice builds up on its wings, then placing your faith in it (flying in icy conditions) is unwise. The wise thing is to believe what the FAA says and to act accordingly. In the same way, we should believe what God has said and act accordingly.

What should we believe?

There are fundamentals of the faith that provide the foundation for everything else in our lives.

So what has God said we should believe? Well, there is much. However, there are a few key things that are crucial to living the Christian life, things that will cause grave problems if not understood or believed. There are more "fundamentals of the faith" than we've listed here. Nevertheless, these cannot be overlooked:

1. The existence of God. Hebrews 11:6 says, "Without faith it is impossible to please Him, for he who comes to God must believe that He is, and that He is a rewarder of those who diligently seek Him." First, we must believe that God exists. The fact is, if we want a satisfactory explanation of the existence of the universe and of the unique nature of humanity, we must believe in God.

2. *The character of God.* Not only must we believe that God exists, we must believe in His perfect character. We must believe that He is good, loving, merciful, kind, just, and patient. If He isn't, then heaven (or someone) help us! If God's character cannot be trusted, then nothing else matters. It is a dangerous world.

3. *The truth of the Scriptures.* If the Bible is not true, we may be in as much hot water as if God did not exist. If the Bible isn't true, we can know nothing for sure. We must trust that God communicated accurately to us in the pages of Scripture. We must accept the Bible at face value when it says that all Scripture is inspired by God, and that it is without error.

4. *The power of God.* Not only must we believe in God's perfect character, but we must believe in His absolute power. If

God's character were not perfect, we could not trust Him to want to do what is best for us. If His power is not absolute, we cannot trust that He is able to do what He wants to do.

5. *Jesus is God.* Jesus claimed to be God. He claimed to be able to forgive sin. He claimed to have risen from the dead. He claims that by believing in Him, we can have eternal life. If that isn't true, then the Bible isn't true, and we have no secure hope.

6. *The Holy Spirit is God.* The Bible claims that the Holy Spirit is God, and that without His ministry to us we cannot live the life God intends us to live.

7. *Humanity is fatally flawed by sin and cannot save itself.* The Bible teaches that all have sinned and come short of the glory of God and the wages of sin are death. There is nothing that humanity can do to make itself acceptable to God. Our only hope is to accept His offer of forgiveness by placing our faith in Jesus and to commit our lives to following Him.

8. *The Christian life is a life of obedience to the will of God.* The Christian abandons his own personal agenda for his life and commits himself as a living sacrifice to God (Rom. 12:1-2).

How can we increase our faith?
We increase our faith by starting where we are and building on that.

I read one time of a suspension bridge that was planned to span a wide gorge out west. Everything about the building of the bridge seemed fairly straightforward except how to get started. Finally, someone came up with an ingenious strategy. They shot an arrow from one side to the other. The arrow carried across the gulf a tiny thread. The thread was used to pull a piece of twine across, the twine pulled after it a small rope, the rope soon carried a cable across, and in time came the iron chains that the bridge was to hang from.

The fact is, the shortest distance between you and the life you long for is total obedience to Christ.

This is much like faith, or any number of things in life that need to be strengthened. Although often weak in its beginning stages, a seemingly small faith can draw us to a stronger and stronger faith that will be used by God in greater and greater ways.

How can we increase our faith? By studying with the Bible and gaining a deeper knowledge of truth, of who God is and what He has said. By praying and by observing the results of obedience and disobedience in your life as well as in the lives of people you know and people in the Bible. Sin never works. Righteousness does. When we come to the point where we deeply believe that, it will strengthen us significantly, because God has built into us an inclination to choose the things we believe will bring us the greatest happiness.

God's way is the best way.

When it comes to faith, many of us are like the man who was walking along a narrow path paying little attention to where he was going. Suddenly he slipped over the edge of a cliff. As he fell, he grabbed a branch growing from the side of the cliff. Realizing that he couldn't hang on for long, he yelled, "Help! Is anybody up there?"

A great, booming voice answered, "Yes, I'm here."

"Who's that?" the man asked.

"The Lord," the great booming voice replied.

"Lord, help me!"

"Do you trust me?"

"Yes, I trust you completely!"

"Then let go of the branch," the Lord said.

"What?!"

"I said, 'Let go of the branch.'"

There was a long pause. Finally, the man yelled, "Is anybody else up there?"

When we get into life's scrapes, when we flounder for direction, when we ache for consolation, when we yearn for fellowship, when we are desperate for deliverance, we cry out to God for help. But then, when the Lord makes it clear what we are to do, we often wonder if there is "*anybody else up there*"*!* There isn't.

God's way is always the best way. The more completely we believe that, the better our lives will go and the more our lives will be a testimony to the grace and sufficiency of the Lord. The *fact* is, the shortest distance between you and the life you long for is total obedience to Christ.

Life-Check

1. How would you have defined faith before you read this chapter? Have you ever been misled in your understanding of the Christian life by a false understanding of faith?

2. In which of the fundamentals of the faith do you feel the strongest? In which do you feel the weakest? Do you think your Christian walk has been hampered by a weak understanding of one of the fundamentals of the faith?

3. How do you think you can strengthen your faith?

For Further Reflection

Scripture

Luke 17:5-6
1 Corinthians 16:13
Hebrews 11:1, 6
Jude 1:3, 20
Romans 12:1-2

Books

Reckless Faith, John MacArthur
30 Days to Understanding What Christians Believe, Max Anders (see "Faith")

21

The Law of Feelings:
Learning to Live with Emotions

Feelings must follow facts and faith,
not lead them.

Whoever has no rule over his own spirit
Is like a city broken down, without walls.
Proverbs 25:28

I'll never forget a story I read in one of James Dobson's books about the value (or lack of it) of misplaced emotions:

It was [many years ago] in a small Oklahoma town which had produced a series of terrible football teams. They usually lost the important games and were invariably clobbered by their arch rivals from a nearby community. Understandably, the students and their parents began to get depressed and dispirited by the drubbing their troops were given every Friday night. It must have been awful.

Finally, a wealthy oil producer decided to take matters in his own hands. He asked to speak to the team in the locker room after yet another devastating defeat. What followed was one of the most dramatic football speeches of all times. This businessman proceeded to offer a brand new Ford car to every boy on the team and to each coach if they would simply defeat their bitter rivals in the next game. Knute Rockne couldn't have said it better.

The team went crazy with sheer delight. They howled and cheered and slapped each other on the [back]. For seven days, the boys ate, drank, and breathed football. At night they dreamed about touchdowns and rumble seats. The entire school caught the spirit of ecstasy, and a holiday fever pervaded the campus. Each player could visualize himself behind the wheel of a gorgeous coupe, with eight gorgeous girls hanging all over his gorgeous body.

Finally, the big night arrived and the team assembled in the locker room. Excitement was at an unprecedented high. The coach made several inane comments and the boys hurried out to face the enemy. They assembled on the sidelines, put their hands together, and shouted a simultaneous "Rah!" Then they ran onto the field and were demolished, thirty-eight to zero.

The team's exuberance did not translate into a single point on the scoreboard. Seven days of hoorah and whoop-de-do simply couldn't compensate for the players' lack of discipline and conditioning and practice and study and coaching and drill and experience and character [and talent]. Such is the nature of emotion. It has a definite place in human affairs, but when forced to stand alone, feelings usually reveal themselves to be unreliable and [quickly passing] and even a bit foolish.[1]

Emotions don't make a good engine. They only make a good caboose. Leading with your emotions is like a boxer leading with his chin. It's only a matter of time until he gets decked. Yet *many* people lead with their emotions much of the time and don't understand why they are always getting knocked facedown on the canvas of life.

We live in a "feel-good" society. We're constantly making decisions based on how we feel at the time, only to pay a dreadful price later on because the truth is, it was a bad decision. Truth is what God says it is, regardless of how we feel.

Emotions don't make a good engine. They only make a good caboose.

Feelings or emotions aren't bad. In the Bible, we see that God has emotions, and that's why we have emotions. We are created in His image. God experiences joy, sorrow, peace, compassion, and anger. So do we. We are emotional beings, and that isn't bad.

So how do we live with our emotions? We must understand them, know their place in the Christian life, and know when to trust them and when not to trust them.

How does God use positive emotions?
God uses positive emotions to enrich our lives.

When we live a life of faithful obedience to God, a life of love, compassion, and forgiveness toward others, we feel enriched and blessed. We experience the fruits of the Spirit, which are love, joy, and peace. The apostle Paul was imprisoned with his friend and fellow-laborer, Silas. Before being jailed, they were arrested, taken before the city officials, and beaten with rods.

The Bible says: "When they had laid many stripes on them, they threw them into prison, commanding the jailer to keep them securely. Having received such a charge, he put them into the inner prison and fastened their feet in the stocks. But at midnight Paul and Silas were praying and singing hymns to God" (Acts 16:23-25).

Paul and Silas had been arrested, humiliated, beaten, and imprisoned, yet they prayed and sang hymns of praise afterward. That is what can happen when one lives in close fellowship with the Lord.

Paul is the same person who was beaten many times, shipwrecked, attacked by animals, stoned and left for dead, yet said that these "light momentary afflictions" were producing an eternal weight of glory far beyond all comparison (2 Cor. 4:16-18). Even in the midst of difficult circumstances, the Lord can give us positive emotions, which make such experiences much easier to deal with.

How does God use negative emotions?
God uses negative emotions to warn us of a need to change something.

Negative emotions, such as unresolved anger, depression, and anxiety can warn us that our life is out of balance, and we need to change something. When David was at the height of his power, he committed adultery with Bathsheba, the wife of one of his greatest generals. Then to cover up the adultery, he had the general killed. It was a flagrant and ghastly abuse of power, which he might have gotten away with. But the eyes of God saw, and David fell under deep conviction by the Holy Spirit. He writes of that experience in Psalm 32:3-5,

> When I kept silent, my bones grew old through my groaning all the day long. For day and night Your hand was heavy upon me; my vitality was turned into the drought of summer. I acknowledged my sin to You, and my iniquity I have not hidden. I said, "I will confess my transgressions to the LORD," and You forgave the iniquity of my sin.

When we sin, God convicts us of that sin, and the terrible negative emotions we feel are intended to get us to repent and change our behavior. In 2 Corinthians 7:10, the apostle Paul wrote, "For godly sorrow produces repentance."

At other times negative emotions are the result of physical problems. Maybe we are ill, or our blood chemistry is out of balance, or medication we're taking has us emotionally off balance. Perhaps we are working too hard, not getting enough rest, eating poorly, or not getting enough exercise. If we cannot discern any spiritual reasons for negative emotions, we need to assess if something physical might be causing them, something we can and should change. When caused by something beyond our control, negative emotions are not pleasant, but neither are they the result of sin for which we need to repent.

How else does God use negative emotions?
God also uses negative emotions to keep us in touch with reality.

There are times when we experience negative emotions even though we haven't sinned. God does not necessarily cause these emotions, but He uses them for good in our lives.

When a loved one dies, for example, we experience deep pain. When we see children on television starving to death or we see bodies broken and lifeless through war, it pains us. We experience that pain not because we sinned but because human life is valuable, and we grieve, as God grieves, at human suffering. The pain we feel keeps us in touch with reality by helping us realize how valuable human life is. It helps us see the world as God sees it and can be used by God to stir us to acts of compassion and evangelism.

Other times when we feel a negative emotion, it may just be because we live in a fallen world. Perhaps our parents abused us, and we don't have the relationship with them that we long for. That's painful, but it's not our fault.

Assuming there is nothing physical interfering with the normal process, if we know the truth (facts), and believe it (faith), and act accordingly, then our emotions (feelings) fall in line. It may take time for injured or damaged emotions to be healed, but they can heal. Just as a caboose goes wherever the engine goes, so our emotions go wherever the facts and our faith take them. If we believe the wrong things, if we act in wrong ways, our emotions will be in turmoil. If we believe the right things, and make the right decisions, our emotions will follow.

This is not to say if you have the truth and make right choices based on truth, your emotions will always be totally pleasant. If the facts are that the road you are traveling is bumpy, then your emotions will feel those bumps. But you can have deep-seated emotional strength and stability even in the midst of circumstantial upheaval.

Take Jesus as an example. On the night in which He was to be betrayed by Judas, He went to the Garden of Gethsemane with His disciples to pray and prepare for the unspeakable horror of the coming hours, when He would suffer and die. In spite of the fact that He was God and knew He would be resurrected, He was, nevertheless, still also a man, and the terror of the coming events overwhelmed Him.

Jesus said to His disciples, "My soul is exceedingly sorrowful, even to death" (Matt. 26:38). He had done nothing wrong, yet He was engulfed in grief.

We live in a fallen world, and even when we believe the right things and make good decisions, we are not exempt from the possibility of great emotional upheaval. Living in fellowship and obedience to God doesn't always lessen the pain we go through, but nevertheless it makes it easier to bear, knowing God is present, that He cares, that He will use everything for good in our lives, that there is purpose and meaning in our pain beyond what we can comprehend.

Emotions must be kept in check if we are

to make good decisions.

I remember the time I wanted some bongo drums. I was walking past a music store with my mother and brother and saw a pair of bongo drums in the window, and something deep within me cried out to own those drums. My desire grew like a fire in a dry house, and before long, my whole life was consumed with getting those drums. I was about thirteen or fourteen years old and had worked at odd jobs long enough to be able to plunk down the rather sizable sum of thirty dollars for them.

Life's order is facts first, then faith, and finally, feelings. Any other order, and the train of life won't run.

Almost the instant I bought them, I knew I had made a mistake. What can you do with bongo drums? I didn't play with a calypso band. I didn't play with *any* band. I took the drums home and by the time I had whacked around on them for thirty minutes, I had exhausted what you can do alone with bongo drums. I put them down and stared at them. Resentment started to build. I began to visualize all the other things I could have bought with that money that would have been fun for a long time. The drums sat around our house unplayed for the next ten years until the drum heads split from old age and my mother got rid of them.

That was a painful but profitable lesson, and it has saved me from many subsequent bad decisions. Whenever I feel an irrational desire for something rise up and grab me by the throat, I scoff at the desire and say, "You're nothing but a set of bongo drums in disguise."

Once or twice since then I failed to heed that warning concerning extreme desire, and I have gotten stung. Once I paid more for a beautiful, newly painted old pickup than I should have. I wanted it, so I didn't investigate it as thoroughly as I should have. The engine blew shortly after I bought it. Because I let my emotions lead me, I got stung again.

When we want something so badly we can't see straight, we are on dangerous ground. We may buy a car that is impractical. We may buy a house that is more than we can afford. We may get emotionally bonded to a person who isn't right for us. All too often we make a mistake. Desire turns to bitterness and despair. All because we allowed ourselves to be led by our emotions, rather than forcing ourselves to follow a good decision-making process.

Make no mistake, it's hard to make the right decisions when you're emotionally involved. But the question is, how much do you want to suffer? Would you rather experience the short-term pain of right decisions, or the long-term pain of wrong decisions? I have learned that lesser pain comes from right decisions.

Emotions . . . no, you can't flat out trust them. They will tell you the truth just often enough to make you think you can trust them. You can't. Life's order is facts first, then faith, and finally, feelings. Any other order, and the train of life won't run.

Life-Check

1. Describe times in your life when you have experienced particularly positive emotions. How did God use them to enrich your life?

2. Describe times in your life when you have experienced particularly negative emotions. What was God trying to warn you of? Do you have any insight on what you might have done to bring the emotions on yourself?

3. Describe times in your life when you have experienced emotional pain due to circumstances beyond your control (death of a loved one, physical illness, etc.). What truth about life was reinforced through that experience?

For Further Reflection

Scripture
1 Corinthians 13:4-7
Galatians 5:22-23
Philippians 4:8-9
Proverbs 25:28
Acts 16:23-25
2 Corinthians 4:16-18
2 Corinthians 7:10

Books
Emotions: Can You Trust Them?, James Dobson
Joy That Lasts, Gary Smally
30 Days to Understanding How To Live as a Christian, Max Anders

How to Teach This Book

*T*his book is useful for truth seekers, for new Christians, and for Christians who want to do a "life-check." In fact, it could be used for a periodic life-check, perhaps each January or on vacation, to help you stay on the right path in life. It is written so that it can be used for small group or discipleship study, as well as for individual study.

If you would like to use the book to teach others, you might find the following guidelines helpful. As you read the guidelines, remember that flexibility is the key to their effective use. You may be leading a high-commitment study or a moderate-commitment study. Use the following suggestions as you think best suit your purpose:

1. Begin your time with prayer.

2. Consider having the participant(s) quote from memory the Scripture passage from the first page of the chapter each week. Or this could also be cumulative. That is, the first week the participants quote the Scripture passage from the first chapter; the second week they quote the central passages from the first two chapters, and so on.
   In small discipleship groups or one-on-one sessions, a higher degree of commitment might be required. In larger groups like a Sunday school class where participation is voluntary, less commitment might be required. Adjust your expectations to the group.

3. At the beginning of the session, summarize the chapter in your own words. You might want to bring in information that was not covered in the book.

4. Discuss the material at the end of the chapters as time per-

mits. Use the information that best fits the group.

5. Have a special time for questions and answers, or just encourage questions during the course of discussion. If you are asked a question to which you don't know the answer (it happens to all of us), just say you don't know, but you'll find out. Then, the following week, you can open the question-and-answer time or the discussion time with the answer to the question from the previous week.

6. Close with prayer.

You may have other things you would like to incorporate. Please feel free to do so. Remember: Flexibility is the key to success. These suggestions are intended as a guide, not a straightjacket.

Notes

Chapter 1

    1. Quoted in John Piper, *Desiring God* (Portland, OR: Multnomah Press, 1986), 15.

    2. Charles Kuralt, *A Life on the Road* (New York: G. P. Putnam's Sons, 1990), 197.

    3. Peggy Noonan, *Life, Liberty, and the Pursuit of Happiness* (Holbrook, MA: Adams Media Corporation, 1994), 214-15.

Chapter 2

    1. James Packer, *Rediscovering Holiness* (Ann Arbor, MI: Servant Publications, 1992), 120.

    2. Ibid, 221.

Chapter 3

    1. Max Anders, *30 Days to Understanding the Bible* (Dallas, TX: Word, Inc., 1994), 233-35. All rights reserved.

Chapter 5

    1. Charles Colson, *A Dangerous Grace* (Dallas: Word Publishing, 1994), 111-12.

Chapter 6

    1. Stephen Covey, *The 7 Habits of Highly Effective People* (New York: Fireside, 1989), 186-87.

Chapter 10

    1. Excerpted with permission from "The Last Great Race" by Gary Paulsen, *Reader's Digest*, March 1994.
Gary Paulsen, *Winterdance* (Orlando, FL: Harcourt, Brace & Co., 1994), 299-301. Used by permission.

Chapter 11

    1. From *Jubilee*, July 1990. Copyright © 1990. Used with permission of Prison Fellowship, P.O. Box 17500, Washington, DC 22041-0500. [pp. 1-3]

Chapter 12

1. Ronald Reagan, *An American Life* (New York: Pocket Books, 1990), 262.

2. Harold Kushner, *When All You Ever Wanted Isn't Enough* (New York: Pocket Books, 1986), 166.

3. William Martin and Jerry Root, eds., *The Quotable Lewis* (Wheaton, IL: Tyndale, 1989), 232.

Chapter 14

1. Quoted in Philip Yancey, *Finding God in Unexpected Places* (Nashville, TN: Moorings, 1995), 153-54.

Chapter 15

1. "Free at Last," *Tabletalk,* October 1989, 12. Used by permission.

2. Ibid.

3. Quoted in Charles Colson, *A Dangerous Grace,* 200-01.

Chapter 17

1. Charles Swindoll, *The Grace Awakening* (Dallas: Word Publishing, 1990), 114-15.

2. Charles Colson, *Faith on the Line* (Wheaton, IL: Victor Publishing, 1994), 97.

Chapter 18

1. Spiros Zodhiates, *The Behavior of Belief: An Exposition of James Based upon the Original Greek Text* (Grand Rapids, MI: Wm. B. Eerdmans, 1966), 26.

2. Quoted in Packer, 270.

3. Ibid, 265-66, 271.

Chapter 19

1. Allan Bloom, *The Closing of the American Mind* (New York: Simon and Schuster, 1987).

Chapter 20

1. For U.S. only: *All Creatures Great and Small,* James Herriot. Copyright © 1972 by James Herriot, St. Martin's Press, Inc., New York, NY. Used by permission. [pp. 314-15]

For English-speaking world outside the U.S.: James Herriot, *All Creatures Great and Small,* Michael Joseph Publishers. Used by permission.

Chapter 21

1. James Dobson, *Emotions: Can You Trust Them?* (Ventura, CA: Regal Books, 1981), 5-6. Used by permission.

About the Author

Dr. Max Anders is a pastor at heart who applies the truths of God's word to people's everyday lives. An original team member with Walk Thru the Bible Ministries and pastor of a megachurch for a number of years before beginning his speaking and writing ministry, Dr. Anders has traveled extensively, speaking to thousands across the country.

His books include the best-selling *30 Days to Understanding the Bible, 30 Days to Understanding How to Live as a Christian, 30 Days to Understanding What Christians Believe,* as well as the ten-volume series *We Believe! The Basics of Christianity.* He holds a Master of Theology degree from Dallas Theological Seminary and a doctorate from Western Seminary in Portland, Oregon.

If you're interested in having Max Anders speak at your conference, church, or special event, please call interAct Speaker's Bureau at 1-800-370-9932.